GOD'S GAME PLAN FOR TEEN BOYS: UNLOCKING YOUR PURPOSE AND CRUSHING LIFE'S CHALLENGES WITH BIBLICAL WISDOM

A FUN, FAITH-FILLED GUIDE TO NAVIGATING THE TEEN YEARS AND BEYOND

NATHANIEL BENNETT

ISBN: 979-8-9988196-9-8 (Paperback) | 979-8-9932062-2-6 (eBook)

Library of Congress Control Number: 2025923170

First Edition: August 2025

Printed in Garden City, Idaho, the United States of America.

Cover & Interior designs by Braeburn & Hope Omnimedia Incorporated.

To my dearest sons, Matthew & Lucas.

"For I know the plans I have for you," declares the Lord,
"plans to prosper you and not to harm you,
plans to give you hope and a future."
–Jeremiah 29:11

CONTENTS

INTRODUCTION

You're in the school hallway, trying to play it cool as you pull up on your crush. You open your mouth, hoping for smooth words, but instead, out comes a jumble of gibberish that would make even a three-year-old cringe. Cue the awkward silence, and voilà—there goes your dignity smashing into a million pieces on the floor. It's the ultimate facepalm moment, and guess what? It doesn't get easier. But hey, don't worry: You're definitely not alone; we've all been there.

Life as a teenage boy is like a video game that no one's bothered to write a tutorial for. The struggle is real, fam. One minute, you're expected to "just be yourself." (Seriously, which version?) The next, you're trying to keep up with all of those Instagram influencers who somehow manage to look like they've stepped straight out of a magazine, making you feel even more like a couch potato.

And as if things aren't already hectic enough, your brain decides to throw in 24/7 dance parties with hormones doing the Harlem Shake. On top of all that noise, adults keep throwing advice at you, like "be confident" or "focus on school." But let's be honest, it feels like they're speaking an alien language. Meanwhile, your go-to life hacks aren't really cutting it anymore. Asking your friends for help is like the blind leading the blind, Googling your problems sucks you into never-ending rabbit holes of weird tips, and pretending everything's fine doesn't change the fact that, well, it's not. Pause. Take a deep breath.

So, here you are, wondering if there's some cheat code for life, a way to make it through these challenges without totally crashing out. The good news? There is, kind of. Enter God's game plan for crushing your teen years. No, it's not boring, and yes, it truly works (mind-blowing revelation, right?). Think of it as the ultimate life advice—powerful, epic, and designed to tackle whatever boss battles get thrown your way.

Now, before you roll your eyes and mentally prepare for another snooze-fest sermon, let me assure you that this book doesn't suck. No cap. It's designed to speak your language and acknowledge the struggles you face daily, offering a fun but deeply rooted guide to walking through life with faith. We're diving into real talk about real issues—dating, peer pressure, finding your purpose, you name it. We'll throw in some biblical wisdom that's relevant to your life, minus the yawns.

Here's the deal: With God as your Player One, you might just find yourself winning in ways you never imagined. Pretty soon, you'll be facing life's challenges like a boss. I'm not promising that you'll suddenly become the world's smoothest talker or crush every math test without breaking a sweat, but I am saying that you're gonna unlock achievements you couldn't have dreamed of. And isn't that what leveling up is all about?

Your mission, should you choose to accept it (and come on, you know you want to), is to dive into this book with an open mind. Maybe gather something to munch on—who doesn't love snacks when embarking on an epic quest? Then, prepare to laugh, learn, and boost your life like never before. Warning: Side effects may include increased awesomeness, newfound confidence, and a stronger faith.

By the end of this book, you'll see that teen life isn't just a series of fails and awkward experiences. Nope, it's also full of potential, growth, and moments where you legit shine. The road might be rocky and unpredictable, but that's what makes the journey worthwhile. And with the right mix of guidance, laughter, and faith, who knows? You might just come out on the other side not just surviving your teen years but thriving in them.

So, take a deep breath, grab a highlighter and journal, and prepare for an adventure that will help transform those epic facepalms into victorious fist pumps. Together, we'll tackle those hallway embarrassments, conquer the video-game-of-life chaos, and discover the secret cheat codes to living your best life in style. Here's to unlocking new levels, embracing growth, and transforming into the person you're destined to become. So, are you ready to trade in your noob status to become God's VIP player? Ready, set, let's go!

———

PART ONE
WHO'S THE REAL MVP? (UNDERSTANDING GOD'S ROLE IN YOUR LIFE)

THE FIRST QUARTER

God never said that the journey would be easy, but He did say that the arrival would be worthwhile. –
Max Lucado

CHAPTER 1
THE ULTIMATE COACH: GETTING TO KNOW GOD

Trust in the Lord with all your heart
and lean not on your own understanding.
–Proverbs 3:5–6

WELCOME to your backstage pass to the mind-blowing magnitude of existence, where you're not just a spectator but an active participant. Here, getting to know God is like going on the ultimate quest for understanding. Forget about battling dragons or decoding ancient scrolls—this adventure is all about uncovering the mysteries of the divine and figuring out how that relates to your own life. Pretty soon, you'll learn that God is basically the ultimate coach: someone who doesn't just see the whole game plan but also knows your every move and celebrates your victories as if they're His own.

In this riveting chapter, we'll spill the deets on things like God's incredible roles as creator and life architect, which might sound like fancy titles for a superhero. But hey, when you think about designing galaxies or orchestrating intricate ecosystems, that analogy doesn't seem too far off! You'll also be invited to think about your unique purpose in life and how it's part of a bigger picture that stretches across time and space. Along the way, we'll peel back the layers of divine identity, showing how God's involvement in our lives isn't just some abstract notion but a tangible reality grounded in love, grace, and intention.

Whether you're tackling tricky homework or trying to figure out your future career path, these insights will transform your everyday struggles into parts of a divinely crafted adventure. So, buckle up and prepare to discover more about the cosmic playbook that includes your very own story.

God as the Creator and Source of Purpose

When it comes to understanding God's role as the ultimate creator, it's like opening the biggest and most exciting puzzle box ever. This is someone who literally planned every galaxy, designed every star, and created every living thing on Earth. That's God for you, the supreme being and source of all things. His creation is not just a random collection of comets and planets scattered in space; oh no, it's an organized universe, crafted with precision and purpose.

God's Plan

When you think about how everything fits together—from the vastness of the galaxies to the most minuscule elements of nature—it's pretty clear that God had a plan right from the start. Every tiny detail speaks volumes about His intention. Look at the way ecosystems work perfectly, with each part fulfilling its role, or the reliability of the sunrise every single day. These are constant reminders of His meticulousness in action. Like an expert architect's blueprint for a grand structure, each component has its place, and without even one, the masterpiece would be incomplete. This thoughtful creation by God is the foundation of our existence and gives each one of us a deep-rooted purpose.

God's Purpose for You

You might wonder how an expanseless universe relates to your life on a personal level. Well, think about it this way: If God took the time to map out something as gigantic and detailed as the universe, imagine how much more thought He's put into your individual journey. The very fact that you are even here means you have a purpose that's been written into the story of creation itself.

This concept is highlighted beautifully in Revelation 4:11 (*New International Version* [*NIV*], 2011/1978), where it states, "You are worthy, our Lord and God, to receive glory and honor and power, for you created all things, and by your will they were created." Your life is more than just a bunch of random events; it's an important part of God's larger picture.

There are so many more insights in Scripture that unpack God's role as the architect of human destiny. Jeremiah 1:5, which declares, "before you were born I set you apart" (*NIV*, 2011/1978), emphasizes this idea, telling us that God knew each person before they were formed, showing that He knew your path long before you came into being. This thoughtful crafting means that your life aligns with God's overall plans. Embracing this knowledge encourages you to see beyond things like chance or coincidence in your life, recognizing that there is a divine purpose behind your journey.

Serving Your Purpose

Reflecting on these aspects can really transform your daily experiences. It shifts your perspective from seeing life as an accident to seeing it as a structured narrative crafted by a loving creator. Take King David. I'm sure we all know who he is, right? (If you don't, you'll meet him in 1 and 2 Samuel in the Old Testament). The story of his life—serving his purpose in his time and then resting with his ancestors—shows how God guides people through their unique roles within their generations. This isn't just something that happens for figures in the Bible; God continues to steer, shape, and unfold each of our stories individually.

Understanding God's continuous involvement in your life might sometimes feel a little bit overwhelming, especially when you're dealing with boring homework or trying to figure out what you want to do with your life. But hear me out: Knowing there's a bigger plan in action should bring you comfort and reassurance rather than stress. Life's ups and downs are like character development plots in your favorite Marvel superhero's origin story, except you're the hero!

Your Unique Purpose

God's detailed blueprint of your life includes an ingrained purpose and meaning. This isn't a "one size fits all" kinda thing but a unique calling made just for you. Colossians 1:16 really sends this message home: "For in him all things were created: Things in heaven and on earth, visible and invisible, whether thrones or powers or rulers or authorities; all things have been created through him and for him" (*NIV*, 2011/1978). This message reinforces your special place in His grand design. Use this realization as motivation to keep moving forward and fuel every decision and action that you take in the pursuit of honoring your role.

Every one of us has a path and purpose that is uniquely intertwined with God's ongoing guidance. While exploring the Bible, you'll find so many examples of diverse callings. Think of Abraham, Moses, or the apostle Paul; they were each assigned particular missions, but all of them were centered around fulfilling God's greater plan. Whether it was leading a nation, liberating a people, or spreading the gospel, each of their stories highlights different parts of God's creative purpose carried out through His guidance.

Embracing God as the ultimate coach and creator will help you face challenges with humor and courage. When you're experiencing doubts or confusion about the direction of your future, remember that God's got the best GPS system ever. There's no better feeling than knowing you're part of a well-thought-out plan, one guided by a loving creator who knows exactly what He is doing. Through everyday activities, decisions, and experiences, God shapes each of our lives intricately, building them into meaningful testimonies that contribute positively to the world.

Understanding Your Identity in Christ

Finding your identity in Christ is like discovering a secret superhero persona—without the tights and cape, obviously. (Unless you're into that. No judgment.) When the world around you is demanding answers about who you are, it's tempting to look at things you've achieved, your drip, or even that fresh new haircut for validation. But the thing is, there's a timeless message waiting to redefine your self-worth: You're crafted in the unique image of God. (Mic drop).

Being made in God's image means you have divine traits etched into your very core. Just as an artist signs their masterpiece, God's signature is on you. Now, this doesn't mean you've had supernatural abilities all along and that they're about to be activated at any moment. (That would be pretty cool though, right?) Rather, it means that you're built with intention, creativity, love, and so much more. This realization can shape how you see yourself and where you find your worth.

But hey, don't think I'm about to prescribe a step-by-step manual on how to find your way through the world because, unlike assembling IKEA furniture, identity isn't a one-time construction project. You need to consistently nurture your bond with God. Strengthening your relationship with Him requires the same dedication you would give to watering and caring for a plant. Daily communication through prayer and connecting with the Bible helps you grow and build your resilience, ensuring that your sense of who you are remains rooted and vibrant.

Faith in Christ

Faith in Christ adds another layer to understanding who you truly are. It's like putting on glasses that let you see life through a different lens. Instead of relying on what you achieve or what others say about you, you start seeing yourself exactly the way that

God does—as valuable and chosen. Your self-perception gets a major upgrade, allowing you to look past your imperfections and focus on the built-in worth that faith gives you. You're no longer defined by the 15 minutes of fame that you may or may not achieve but by the unwavering love and acceptance found in your relationship with God.

The teachings found in the Bible have a whole bunch of totally game-changing ideas about rebirth through a connection with Christ. Think of it as hitting the reset button on life. For example, when Paul writes in 2 Corinthians 5:17 that anyone who places their faith in Christ is a new creation, he's saying that anyone can get a cosmic do-over. All those past mistakes—yes, that includes the awkward photo from last year's school dance—and moments of doubt become overshadowed by the light of a fresh beginning. It's a soul-deep transformation that's meant to shift your mindset and future actions.

The Body of Christ

Being part of Christ's body—not literally—means you're joining an awe-inspiring community, one that's filled with people who've likely experienced the same sense of wonder, confusion, and growth spurts you're going through. Belonging to this community shows you that you don't walk this journey alone. Everyone has a role to play, much like pieces of a puzzle that fit together to reveal a bigger picture. You're not only valued individually but also collectively, and you enrich the group of believers with your distinct story.

Exploring God's Character and Love

You're in the middle of a seemingly endless math class, dying for a little bit of excitement or discovery. Hold up! You're about to get what you asked for. Here's something that's way more exciting than algebra equations—getting to know God and understanding His amazing qualities. Brace yourself because we're about to head into an adventure that doesn't require a calculator, just a curious heart.

Let's start with three of God's jaw-dropping characteristics:

- **Omnipotence:** This means He's all-powerful, in other words, stronger than any morning coffee you've ever had. You know those times when you lift a heavy backpack and feel like you've just pulled Excalibur from the stone? Multiply that by infinity, and you're still nowhere near God's strength. He's the unbeatable force behind every spectacular sunrise and breathtaking mountain.
- **Omniscience:** It can be both comforting and a little intimidating to realize there's someone who gets you better than anyone else. But that's the thing about God: He knows everything. Yes, everything. From the number of hairs on your head (even when you were rocking those wild hairdos you don't want to talk about) to the mysteries of the universe, nothing escapes His attention. He's the most knowledgeable person ever, even smarter than the kid who aces every test without studying.
- **Omnipresence:** No matter where you are—whether you're just chilling in your room, hanging with friends, or maybe stuck at a boring family reunion—God is there, too. His presence is like Wi-Fi that never fails, providing

a constant connection that's always available, even when life feels like it's buffering.

But how do we experience God's presence in our day-to-day lives? Well, life is full of amazing moments that scream His handiwork. Have you ever marveled at a magnificent rainbow after a storm or felt such a deep sense of peace in chaos? These are divine nudges, reminding you of His active participation in your life.

God's Love and Grace

Now, let's get the low-down on God's incredible expressions of love and grace. A. W. Tozer (2017) nails it when he says that grace is about God's goodness directed toward humans despite our faults. Think of it this way: Grace is like your favorite teacher giving you another chance after you totally bombed the final. It's a gift freely given, not one based on credit.

Jesus Christ is literally the ultimate expression of this unconditional love. He's the friend who takes the blame for something you did, allowing you to walk free. The Bible tells us that God's love is eternal, sovereign, unchanging, and infinite. It's a love that ignores boundaries and leaps over hurdles, reaching out to embrace us exactly where we are.

———

EXERCISE: MINDSET PRACTICE
GOD'S HIGHLIGHT REEL

Psalm 19:1 reminds us that God's character is visible in His creation: "The heavens declare the glory of God; the skies proclaim the work of his hands" (NIV, 2011/1978). Use this verse as inspiration to embrace something I like to call "God's highlight reel."

When you focus on specific moments where His presence was undeniable—a sunny surprise during a gloomy day or a kind word when you needed it—you train your mind to recognize His influence in daily life. **This mindset practice can change your outlook and reinforce your identity in powerful ways.**

For this exercise, I want you to look for God's presence in your daily life. You might be shook by how much He's showing up throughout the day without you even realizing it.

01

For the next five days, write down one way you've seen God's character or love displayed in your life or the world around you.

02

At the end of the week, review your "highlight reel" and reflect on how these observations shape your understanding of God.

By the end of this exercise, you'll see that **God is constantly revealing Himself**; you just need to pay attention.

EXERCISE: MINDSET PRACTICE
GOD'S HIGHLIGHT REEL

Question: How have you seen God's character or love displayed
in your life or the world around you?

DAY 1

DAY 2

DAY 3

DAY 4

DAY 5

My understandings are...

Question: How have these
observations shape your
understanding of God?

☥ EQ EXERCISE: EMOTION EXPLORER

You know how eating pizza satisfies your cravings? Experiencing divine love is like chowing down on a spiritual soul-food feast. It fills voids, eases anxieties, and gives you a sense of belonging. You're reminded that you're never alone, no matter how lonely life might sometimes feel. Philippians 4:6 is a great reminder of this, stating, "Do not be anxious about anything, but in every situation, by prayer and petition, with thanksgiving, present your requests to God" (NIV, 2011/1978).

I want you to keep these words in mind as we get into this next exercise, which is all about reframing your perspective through God's eyes. Follow these steps:

1) Next time you find yourself facing a challenge, identify your emotions. You might want to write down the situation and how it's affecting you in your journal.

2) Ask yourself: How would God view this situation?

3) Practice reframing your perspective based on everything you've learned about God's character and how it's defined by love, wisdom, and patience.

When you repeat this exercise, you'll see how embracing God's love can influence your emotional health.

Witnessing God's love can also transform your personal relationships. Think of how forgiveness, patience, and empathy—the building blocks of healthy connections—are all reflections of divine love. When you can wrap your head around God's grace, it'll really get you right in the feels, making you kinder and more understanding toward others. You'll be able to boost both your own well-being and the happiness of those around you. It's totally a win-win!

LET'S BRING IT IN

As we wrap up this deep dive into understanding God's nature and our relationship with Him, remember that life is the coolest puzzle you've ever tackled. Each piece—whether it's one of your ups, downs, or super boring moments—fits perfectly into a grand design crafted by the ultimate creator. Every sunrise you see is God's daily reminder of how thoughtfully He's organized this universe, and yes, that includes your personal journey, too. Next time you're stuck wondering why a school project feels so tough or why life's got you on the ropes, just take a deep breath. Trust that God is guiding you through every twist and turn, steering your unique story toward something greater than you can imagine.

In your walk with God, you're not just any NPC but a hero in your own right. Whether you're dealing with the confusion of growing up, deciding which classes to pick, or figuring out your place in the world, God is right there with His next-level strength and wisdom. And the best part? You're never alone. The universe isn't just about stars and planets; it's about you having a spot, a purpose within this amazing masterpiece. So, dare to embrace this adventure, knowing that there's love, direction, and joy at every step. Who knew your deepest identity was rooted in something as cool as being handcrafted by the greatest creator ever?

CHAPTER 2
YOUR SPIRITUAL PLAYBOOK: WHY THE BIBLE MATTERS

All Scripture is God-breathed and is useful for teaching,
rebuking, correcting and training in righteousness.
–2 Timothy 3:16–17

HANDLING life's twists and turns with the Bible as your playbook is like unlocking hidden levels in your favorite video game. Each new quest is packed with challenges that can turn you into a fearless life warrior, all with the help of a trusty sidekick who knows the best shortcuts and has your back when you're up against the ultimate boss battles. Whether it's dealing with never-ending high school drama, deciding between joining the soccer team and debate club, or tackling those major decisions about your future, this chapter arms you with wisdom straight out of ancient scrolls.

We'll unfold the stories and wisdom buried within those sacred pages, showing you how to use them as practical tools for everyday life. Think of it as assembling an arsenal of virtues—kindness, honesty, resilience—that make even the toughest decisions a no-brainer. You'll see how Scripture can be your personal compass, guiding you through various crossroads and dilemmas. You'll also discover how biblical teachings are super-relevant tools for making choices and growing as a person, not outdated lessons.

Using Scripture for Personal Growth

Trying to find your way in life can sometimes feel like trying to play a video game without a guide. Luckily, you've got the ultimate spiritual handbook—the Bible—to help tackle those tricky levels called "life decisions." Using Scripture equips you with a divine cheat code for decision-making and also unlocks personal growth as you face new challenges and experiences.

Making Value-Reflecting Decisions

Let's face it: Daily life throws up choices that require more than just gut instinct. Here's where the Bible steps in as an invaluable tool for making value-reflecting decisions. It's a moral compass linked with divine wisdom, guiding you through the maze of life.

Let's say you're at a crossroads: One path seems easy, while the other looks rough, but you know it will be more rewarding. By drawing ideas from biblical principles, you can match your choices up with values like humility, love, and integrity. Just like Proverbs 15:22 speaks about seeking advice, using Scripture for decision-making helps ensure your purpose succeeds by aligning your thoughts with God's greater plan (Abimbola, 2024).

A Shelter From the Storm

Beyond decisions, life's challenges can sometimes make you feel as though you're stuck in a storm without an umbrella. That's when the Bible offers reassurance and motivation. It's basically like having a homie constantly whispering words of encouragement whenever doubts start to creep in. During tough times, God's voice resonates through Scripture, reminding us of His omnipresence.

Take Jeremiah 29:11, for example, which reassures us of God's plans for peace and hope even when circumstances seem grim: "'For I know the plans I have for you,' declares the Lord, 'plans to prosper you and not to harm you, plans to give you hope and a future'" (*NIV*, 2011/1978). Similarly to the comfort of a warm blanket wrapped around you during a thunderstorm, it gives you the motivation you need to keep pushing forward.

Trust Your Struggle

Real talk, the power of biblical stories is pretty OP. They cause us to reflect on our personal values and inspire both emotional and moral revamps. Let's look at Joseph's story in Genesis 37–50; it's a classic tale of redemption and perseverance. Who would've thought that going from prison to a palace could mirror God's overall plan? Despite the setbacks, Joseph's unwavering trust in God turned him into a leader who saved nations from famine. This story encourages us to think about how our own trials sculpt our character, aligning us more closely with Christ's image (Abimbola, 2024).

Anchored in Christ

The Bible also shows us that the essence of resilience isn't just enduring trials. It's more like a muscle; the more you work it, the stronger it gets. Remember the many ways Paul faced persecution in the Book of Acts? Instead of giving up, he exercised his resilience muscle and showed that true perseverance comes from leaning on Scripture. Through all of his struggles, Paul's faith stayed strong, showcasing how life's challenges actually strengthened his dedication to God's Word. His example reassures us that hardships are opportunities to grow in faith and that relying on the Bible as our solid foundation can empower us through each storm.

No doubt about it, traveling this earthly plane is challenging, but biblical wisdom will show you how to weather your struggles with strength and grace. Connecting with God's Word regularly is what bolsters your inner resolve. In the midst of modern-day chaos, immersing yourself in Scripture gives you some much-needed clarity and peace—a bit like finding an oasis in a desert. By anchoring yourself in the Bible's teachings, you discover the quiet strength needed to weather any crisis with the knowledge that God's promises are steadfast.

Trust in God's Guidance

When you're tempted to do everything on your own, Proverbs 3:5–6 is a powerful reminder to trust in God's wisdom: "Trust in the Lord with all your heart and lean not on your own understanding; in all your ways submit to him, and he will make your paths straight" (*NIV*, 2011/1978). Reading these words, you can imagine God saying, "Chill, I've got this."

This verse encourages you to have faith in God's understanding rather than only relying on your brainpower. Think of it as using Google Maps versus just trying to remember directions from that one time you drove through town with your 'rents. Following God's lead keeps your path straighter, clearer, and less likely to feature metaphorical traffic jams.

You Gotta Have Faith

Now, let's talk about faith. This isn't just a cool collectible card you keep in your back pocket. Rather, think of it as the engine in your car—it keeps the whole thing moving forward. When you prioritize divine guidance over self-reliance, something magical happens: Your relationship with God grows stronger. Sort of like bonding with your best buddy over late-night pizza and video games, it helps kick doubt to the curb, leaving you cruising smoothly down life's highway.

Avengers Assemble!

Then there's Philippians 4:13 (*NIV*, 2011/1978): "I can do all this through him who gives me strength." This is a reminder that you can face anything life throws your way with God's strength on your side. Whether it's acing an exam or handling friendship drama, tapping into God's power gives you the confidence boost you need. Plus, knowing you're not alone in your battles keeps you humble. It's like joining forces with an all-star team, where each member brings their unique strengths to conquer whatever comes their way.

A Problem Shared

Community support is pretty game-changing, too. God's

wisdom often shines through the people we meet along the way. Sharing your struggles with friends or mentors can give you the fresh perspectives and advice you need to navigate rough waters. It's like teaming up for a group project, except here, everyone contributes, making the task more manageable and enjoyable. Having a supportive squad around helps remind you that you're never truly alone, even when life feels like an unsolvable math problem.

Embrace Challenges

And let's not forget the joy of trials. Yes, I said joy! Okay, so let's pretend that life is one of those giant obstacle courses you'd find on *American Ninja Warrior*, minus the splashy water hazards. James 1:2–4 (*NIV*, 2011/1978) nudges us to see this challenge as an opportunity for growth:

Consider it pure joy, my brothers and sisters, whenever you face trials of many kinds, because you know that the testing of your faith produces perseverance. Let perseverance finish its work so that you may be mature and complete, not lacking anything.

Like discovering a hidden treasure chest in a dungeon crawl, these difficulties, believe it or not, can bring deep satisfaction once you overcome them. Sure, looking at challenges as joyful experiences sounds crazy, but it's like nailing a tough new skating skill—it gets easier, and you become more resilient. The more obstacles you face head-on, the better you get at the game of life, building steadfastness along the way.

Looking at the bigger picture helps anchor you during life's storms. Keeping your eyes on the prize, knowing that these trials, though tough, pave the road to something greater, is comforting. Your faith is your sturdy anchor, holding you firm against the stormy seas. It's reassuring to know that every struggle is part of a larger story, one that's ultimately filled with hope and promises of brighter days ahead.

———

EXERCISE: COACH'S CORNER

Reflect on Philippians 4:13 (NIV, 2011/1978): "I can do all things through him who gives me strength." Then, discuss the following with a parent or mentor:

1. Share a moment when you felt God's presence in your life.

2. What qualities of God do you admire most?

3. How can your parent/mentor support your spiritual journey?

INTROSPECTIVE JOURNALING
My BIBLE JOURNEY

In the Bible, 2 Timothy 3:16 (NIV, 2011/1978) states that "All Scripture is God-breathed and is useful for teaching, rebuking, correcting and training in righteousness." This emphasizes the value and purpose of Scripture, which is the goal of this exercise.

In your journal, reflect on the following prompts:

1. Write about your current relationship with the Bible.

2. Describe any challenges or doubts you have about Scripture.

3. Set goals for how you want to engage with the Bible moving forward.

LET'S BRING IT IN

So, there you have it—using the Bible as a resource can make all those tough decisions a little less daunting. It's the ultimate player's guide, and when it's tucked away in your back pocket, it can help you face not just the major crossroads but also the tiny forks in your path that pop up daily. Now that you know more about its lessons, tales, and nuggets of wisdom, you're all set to grow from the inside out, building a character that's sturdy enough to tackle whatever level life throws your way. Think of it as gaining experience points every time you solve a puzzle or win a boss battle.

But let's not forget that life's an unpredictable game. Sometimes, you'll face dragons you didn't expect or enter deserts without clear pathways. That's where faith hops into the copilot seat. Learning to lean on God's wisdom is the key to activating your spiritual GPS when you hit a dead end. Plus, you've got a team—a community offering support and advice faster than you can say, "Avengers assemble!" Embrace each challenge with humor and courage, knowing they're all chances to level up and become the epic hero of your own story. Now, go forth and conquer, young knight!

CHAPTER 3
PRE-GAME WARM-UP: DEVELOPING A PRAYER LIFE

Do not be anxious about anything, but in every situation,
by prayer and petition, with thanksgiving,
present your requests to God.
–Philippians 4:6

DEVELOPING a prayer life is like gearing up for an epic game where the playing field is your mind and heart. This isn't a game of chance but one that requires strategy and commitment, much like mastering a new guitar chord or perfecting a skateboarding trick. When it comes time to dive into a match, instead of warming up with jumping jacks or dribbling drills, you prep by connecting with God. Getting ready doesn't come without its challenges; at first, it might feel as awkward as reaching for the first slice of pizza on a date, but soon enough, you'll discover it's a whole lot more rewarding than scoring the winning goal.

In this chapter, we're going to explore how prayer can become your secret weapon against life's pressures. You'll learn how making the

Bible a part of your daily routine equips you with the wisdom and strength of a guidebook filled with timeless strategies and secret passwords. We'll also dig into different types of prayer, showing you how each one forms part of an all-purpose toolkit for fixing whatever comes your way. From discovering how to create a consistent prayer routine to using emotional prayer mapping as a tool for better mental health, you'll encounter a whole playbook of new faith-based tactics.

Connecting With the Bible and God

The first step in developing a next-level prayer life is making the Bible a cornerstone of your life by integrating it into your daily routine. In Chapter 2, you got to know this sacred text a little better. You saw that it isn't just an ancient scroll filled with dos and don'ts but that it's basically an action plan to help tackle the real challenges you face every day. It allows you to face school assignments, friendship dramas, or sports pressure armed with wisdom from the ages—sounds awesome, right?

The Ultimate Search Engine

Reading the Bible effectively means approaching it not just as a book but as a living conversation starter with God. At the same time, you could think of it as the ultimate search engine, always ready to give you advice for every life situation. You can start by finding passages that relate directly to what you're experiencing. Say you're feeling anxious about an upcoming test —turn to Scriptures that talk about peace and trust (for example, 1 Peter 5:7). If you want to make reading it a thrilling quest, try diving deeper into contexts, just like you'd investigate the stats before a big game or Google a fact you're curious about.

Get Inspired

Now, onto using the Bible as a practical guide for life's hurdles. You see, it's packed with real-life stories, instructions, and promises that won't steer you wrong. Whenever you're faced with tricky dilemmas or a crossroads, look for characters who've been through similar trials. Their epic tales offer lessons on courage, decision-making, and handling setbacks. Ever heard about David and Goliath? I mean, who hasn't, right? But that story isn't just about slingshots and Philistine; it's about faith and standing up against overwhelming odds. Get inspired, apply those principles to your own "giants," and watch how they fall.

Types of Prayer

Moving on to the array of types of prayer. Yep, there are types! Each serves a purpose and helps you connect with God on a different level, but they can all take the form of heart-to-heart talks with Him. Let's look at some of them:

- First, there's praise, which is all about giving God a high-five for who He is.
- Then, thanksgiving is when you express gratitude for your wins and blessings, even those you didn't expect.
- Petitioning is asking for help—whether it's for guidance, passing that all-important exam, or just getting a handle on those overwhelming teenage emotions.
- Lastly, intercession involves praying for others: showing love by lifting their needs to God.

Now, developing a consistent prayer routine might sound like a chore, but it's really more like setting a regular hangout time with a best friend. Starting your morning with Scripture and prayer sets your day off on a positive note. Keeping a journal where you write out prayers and reflect on passages you read is another great way to connect with your faith—maybe try that in the evenings if you're not a morning person.

Consistency doesn't mean rigidly sticking to one thing no matter what, though. Go ahead and mix it up! Try journaling one day, walking while talking to God another, or even doodling prayers when you're hit with writer's block. The important thing here is manageability—keep it simple and suited to your life's rhythm.

Figuring out how to fit these practices into your already-hectic daily life can seem like a lot, but patience and persistence really do pay off. Creating a space—a quiet corner or a special spot in the garden—dedicated to praying and reading can help get you into a routine. Keeping some visual reminders like sticky notes with motivational verses around your house or photos on your phone can encourage you to keep connecting with Scripture.

Memorizing encouraging verses can also strengthen your mind with God's truths, throwing you some hope when the struggle gets real. One great option to start with is Proverbs 3:5–6, which states, "Trust in the Lord with all your heart and lean not on your own understanding; in all your ways submit to him, and he will make your paths straight" (*NIV*, 2011/1978).

Another awesome way to stay in touch with Scripture is by discussing it with friends. Sharing what you've learned, asking questions, and spilling the tea on all your latest findings during study-group meetups can create stronger bonds over shared beliefs. Plus, hearing different perspectives gives you a deeper under-standing of biblical teachings, helping you see some relevance and applications to your own life that you might've missed. The togeth-erness formed in these sessions reinforces accountability and encourages you to apply the principles you're learning about to everyday life.

Prayer Goes With Everything

Incorporating prayer into everyday life can feel like trying to catch a greased pig in a rodeo; it's tricky, slippery, and might leave you questioning your life choices. But don't stress! I'm here to help break it down for you and show you how fun it actually is.

———

MINDSET PRACTICE: PRAYER MVP
MOST VALUABLE PRACTICE

Mix It Up

First off, it's all about mixing things up. Sticking to one method of prayer is like eating the same cereal every day—you could do it, but eventually, it'll get pretty lame. Instead, try experimenting with different methods for a week. Write a few lines in a journal one day, then take a meditative walk or express yourself through art the next. This way, you'll discover what fits you best while still maintaining constant communication with God.

Rate and Reflect

Once you've given a few different methods a spin, it's time to rate each one. Break out your inner critic and pretend you're a judge on America's Got Talent. When you try these different approaches, think about how they make you feel and how close they bring you to God. Are you feeling peaceful and connected after your walk, or was doodling while praying your idea of divine bliss? Keep track because this will help you develop a personalized prayer routine that fits you as well as your favorite pair of sneakers.

Make It Personal

Developing a personalized prayer routine is like building your ultimate playlist on Spotify. You've got your favorite beats lined up, from vibey anthems to those mellow tunes that help chill you out. The goal is the same: creating a daily conversation with God that's custom-made just for you. Maybe your perfect mix includes morning journaling, lunchtime art therapy, and evening walks. The aim is to stick with it; soon enough, it will become a part of who you are.

EQ EXERCISE: EMOTIONAL PRAYER MAPPING

Let's take a sec to talk about emotional prayer mapping. It's like venting to your most understanding friend about what's been killing your vibe, but this time, you're chatting with the Big Guy upstairs. Whether you're feeling as high as a kite or as low as the bass on your favorite track, expressing your emotions to God is more important than keeping everything bottled up. After all, nobody wants to be a pressure cooker just waiting to blow.

Take a Beat

Taking a moment to reflect on your emotions at the end of the day is more important than you might think. Consider doing this during a quiet moment before bed, when the world has slowed down and you're left alone with your thoughts. Get comfortable and consider what feelings dominated your day. Did anger rear its ugly head, or were you hyped up with joy? Take a moment for each emotion, say a short prayer, and thank God for listening. This simple act can do wonders for your overall well-being and emotional stability.

Here's a little cheat sheet I cooked up that you can use to get the ball rolling:

- Anger Prayer
- Anxiety Prayer
- Frustration Prayer
- Insecurity Prayer
- Sadness Prayer

⟟ EQ EXERCISE:
EMOTIONAL PRAYER MAPPING

Anger Prayer

Anger can sometimes feel like that annoying song you can't get out of your head. Trust me, I get it. Sometimes, life can just get too much, especially when you're feeling disrespected or misunderstood by your parents or teachers at school. Or maybe you and your homies are on the outs, so you're not sure if you're still welcome at their lunch table. Let's not forget all of that stress and pressure to perform well in school. Next time you start seeing red, try this prayer out:

"Lord, I'm feeling angry and frustrated right now.

Help me to control my temper and respond with wisdom.

Your word says, 'A gentle answer turns away wrath,

but a harsh word stirs up anger' (NIV, 2011/1978, Proverbs 15:1).

Give me the strength to be gentle, even when I'm upset.

I know You understand my anger and don't condemn me for it.

Empower me to channel this energy into positive actions.

With Your help, I can turn this moment of anger into

an opportunity for growth and understanding."

☘ EQ EXERCISE:
EMOTIONAL PRAYER MAPPING

Anxiety Prayer

If you feel like you're constantly a nervous wreck, don't beat yourself up about it, bro. You're definitely not alone: 36% of teens say they feel anxious or nervous because of stress (Adolescent Psychiatry Staff, 2021). I mean, you have so much on your plate right now. You're probably worried about the future and trying to figure out college decisions or your career path. The fear of failure can really get you in your feels, too, but you don't need to let it get you down. When those anxieties start creeping up on you again, repeat this prayer:

"God, my heart is racing with worry about the future. I'm scared about [specific concern]. Please calm my fears. Remind me of Your promise: 'Do not be anxious about anything, but in every situation, by prayer and petition, with thanksgiving, present your requests to God' (NIV, 2011/1978, Philippians 4:6). I trust in Your plan for me. Wrap me in Your peace that surpasses all understanding. You've given me the power to overcome this anxiety through Your strength. I look forward with hope, knowing that You hold my future in Your loving hands."

🕴 EQ EXERCISE:
EMOTIONAL PRAYER MAPPING

Frustration Prayer

We all get frustrated from time to time, right? I mean, with all those hormones doing you dirty, it gets pretty tough to control your impulses or express how you feel. Sometimes, you low-key wanna crash out, but then you remember that everyone expects you to just "be a man." Well, instead of bottling that frustration, maybe you can try this prayer out instead:

"Heavenly Father, I'm feeling so frustrated with [specific situation]. It seems like nothing is going right. Help me remember Your words: 'Let us not become weary in doing good, for at the proper time we will reap a harvest if we do not give up' (NIV, 2011/1978, Galatians 6:9). Give me patience and perseverance. Comfort me with the knowledge that this frustration is temporary. You've equipped me with the ability to overcome these challenges, and I'm hopeful that through this struggle, I'll emerge stronger and wiser."

♟ EQ EXERCISE:
EMOTIONAL PRAYER MAPPING

Insecurity Prayer

Can I tell you a secret? Everyone gets insecure. Yes, even your favorite TikTok influencer. It's not surprising that you might be feeling this way, not with all the physical changes you're experiencing and the urge to constantly compare yourself to the people around you and online. Maintaining an image is hard, bro. But you don't need to shoulder this struggle alone. Try using this prayer the next time an Insta post makes you feel some type of way:

"Dear God, I'm feeling insecure about [specific insecurity]. Sometimes, I don't feel good enough. Remind me of Your love and that I am fearfully and wonderfully made. Your word says, 'For we are God's handiwork, created in Christ Jesus to do good works' (NIV, 2011/1978, Ephesians 2:10). Help me see myself through your eyes. Comfort me with the assurance that my worth comes from You, not others' opinions. You've empowered me with unique gifts and talents, and I'm filled with hope knowing that You have great plans for my life."

⭐ EQ EXERCISE:
EMOTIONAL PRAYER MAPPING

Sadness Prayer

It's okay to not be okay. I want you to remember that. Maybe you've lost someone you care about, either through their passing away or a rough breakup. Maybe you're just low-key feeling lonely or like a total social pariah. You can take your sadness to God, too; you don't need to hold onto it all by yourself. When you do need to let it out, try this prayer:

"Lord, my heart is heavy with sadness because of [your specific reason]. I feel alone and hurt. Comfort me with Your presence. Your word promises, 'The Lord is close to the brokenhearted and saves those who are crushed in spirit' (NIV, 2011/1978, Psalm 34:18). Help me feel Your closeness and find hope in You. Wrap Your loving arms around me and remind me that this pain won't last forever. You've given me the strength to endure and grow through this sadness. I look forward with hope, knowing that joy will come in the morning."

EQ EXERCISE:
EMOTIONAL PRAYER MAPPING

Sharing your emotions with God doesn't mean you have to lay everything bare in one go; start small. Like a gardener planting seeds, sprinkle in little prayers throughout your day. If you're having a bad time dealing with a homie who's grumpier than a cat getting a bath, send up a quick request for patience and peace. These small moments of connection build a spiritual foundation strong enough to weather any storm.

The beauty of mixing prayer into your daily life lies in its power to transform how you experience your emotions. Have you ever noticed that sharing a funny story with a friend somehow makes it funnier? It's the same with prayer. By bringing your emotions to God, you're not simply offloading them; you're acknowledging them, embracing them, and finding strength in your vulnerability.

LET'S BRING IT IN

Let's be real: Life can often be a chaotic whirlwind of tests, friendship stress, and those endless chores your parents keep reminding you about. In this chapter, we've explored how building a connection with God through prayer and Scripture is like finding a secret weapon against all that anxiety. It's basically a direct line to the Big Guy who knows all the answers and has designed the bigger picture. By mixing Bible reading into your routine, you're unlocking tips and tricks to tackle everything from nerves before a test to feeling ghosted at lunch. Each story and verse becomes part of your playbook, helping you level up your courage and peace.

Now, as we wrap up, remember that prayer isn't about following strict rules or turning into a monk. It's more like hanging out with your best friend, except this bro's always available no matter what time it is. Whether you're writing out thoughts in a journal, sketching your prayers, or taking a beat during that rowdy bus ride home, you're connecting with God on a personal level. So, when life throws you curveballs, you've got your spiritual toolbox ready to hook you up with some calm and clarity. Ultimately, the goal is to create a daily rhythm that's as natural as breathing—your way of inviting peace, one prayerful pause at a time.

CHAPTER 4
LIVING OUT YOUR FAITH: BEING A LIGHT IN THE WORLD

For you created my inmost being;
you knit me together in my mother's womb.
–Psalm 139:13

YOU WOULDN'T LEAVE a superhero suit hanging in the closet, would you? Similarly, you shouldn't keep your faith tucked away. Living according to your Christian values adds a splash of color to the canvas of life. It gives you the opportunity to step out boldly, knowing that there's an adventure waiting to unfold when you let every action reflect what you believe and when you allow those beliefs to shape how you show up on the daily. See, faith is more than just a personal conviction—it's a beacon that lights up the world around you. Each kind gesture or moment of empathy can create ripples that go far beyond your immediate circle, bringing warmth to those who might need it most.

In this chapter, I'm going to show you how to turn that internal spark of belief into actionable steps you can take in everyday life.

You'll discover ways to face challenges with grace and stand firm in the midst of peer pressure without losing sight of who you truly are. We'll dive into stories and insights that encourage you to serve others selflessly while making sure your light doesn't just shine but dazzles. By the end, you'll see how everyday acts of kindness can light up a path not just for yourself but for everyone who comes across you.

Faith in Action

Your faith is a lot like your favorite hoodie—it's comfy and familiar, and it's meant to be worn out in the world, where it can make a real difference. Living your faith means acting on it, and that's when things get interesting. Let's see how.

Faith Is a Verb

True faith isn't just about what you believe; it's about what you do. Imagine if superheroes only talked about their powers but never actually used them. Super lame, right? Beliefs are important, but actions are what turn those beliefs into something that others can see and feel. We can see this idea reflected in the teachings of Jesus, who emphasized that love and faith go hand in hand through our actions. When you show kindness, offer help, or simply listen to someone who needs an ear, you're demonstrating God's love in a tangible way.

Now, how can you practice these actions in your everyday life? That's where identifying opportunities comes in. Life throws endless chances at us to spread positivity and light. Whether it's smiling at a stranger, helping a homie out with their homework, or sticking up for someone who's being bullied instead of whipping out your phone to record it, these choices matter. They're moments where you get to be a beacon of positivity to the people around you. You don't need superpowers to make someone's day brighter; you just need to be present and willing.

Serving Others Selflessly

Loving your neighbor doesn't mean just mowing their lawn—unless they ask, then maybe consider it! Selfless service can take the form of volunteering at a local food bank or organizing a charity event at school. It involves putting others before yourself, which is a lot easier than it sounds. Trust me, I know. And let's face it, being selfless might not always be glamorous, but it sure does build character.

The cool thing is that serving others isn't just about big gestures. Sprinkling everyday activities with a spirit of kindness and compassion can have a powerful impact. It's the small things—holding the door open, saying "thank you," or checking in on a buddy—that reinforce a culture of care. It's a bit like planting seeds; you never know which tiny action will grow into something bigger.

Here's some guidance to keep in mind while exploring ways to demonstrate God's love through actions:

- Start by looking around you: Who needs help? What needs fixing? How can you contribute positively?
- Try volunteering once a month or making it a goal to do at least one kind thing each day.

The key is consistency and intention. As you practice intentional acts of kindness, you become a vessel for God's love, spreading warmth wherever you go.

Another aspect is recognizing that there's no one-size-fits-all approach to showing love through actions. It's a personal journey that reflects your unique personality and strengths. Maybe you're great at cooking, so you prepare meals for someone who's struggling. Or maybe you're the GOAT at math, so you tutor classmates without expecting anything in return. These all count as vibrant expressions of your faith.

Lastly, don't shy away from turning everyday tasks into acts of service. It's not complicated to transform boring moments into meaningful ones. Doing chores without being asked, listening when your parents need to vent, or spending time with a younger sibling can all reflect God's love.

Navigating Challenges

In a world swirling with challenges and temptations, maintaining your integrity while surrounded by adversity is like trying to keep your ice cream cone upright on a scorching summer day—you've got to be vigilant! As teenage boys, you're at a unique crossroads where peer pressure can easily steer you off course. But don't sweat it, fam; I've got you. There are so many strategies you can use to swerve the drama without letting go of what's important to you.

Peer Pressure

So, you're standing in a room full of people who think it's cool to ditch class for a quick trip to the mall. Or maybe you're being pushed to stay out past curfew even though you know it's against the rules. It might feel like everyone is expecting you to throw up deuces to your values, but here's the thing: You don't have to. You just need to have a game plan, kind of like knowing when to pivot in basketball when someone's about to steal the ball from you.

Start by anticipating situations where peer pressure might roll up and prepare yourself with responses that are assertive but respectful. Something as simple as saying, "Nah, I'm good," when offered something you're uncomfortable with can be incredibly powerful. Also, consider finding a buddy, a partner in integrity, so to speak, who shares your values—strength in numbers isn't just for Marvel movies.

Handling the Haters

You might find yourself being laughed at for sticking to your beliefs, like if you choose attending church over watching the big game. In times like these, humor can be your secret weapon. A light joke or funny comment can chill tension and show others that you're confident in your identity. For example, if someone mocks your choice to go to youth group, you could reply, "Well, somebody has to keep their halo shiny!" Staying light-hearted doesn't minimize your beliefs; it shows resilience and self-assurance.

Growing Through Experience

Resilience is like your personal force field, keeping negativity at bay. One way to strengthen it is through prayer or meditation. Taking time each day to connect with God can give you the peace and strength you'll need to face any challenge.

Connecting with Scripture is another fantastic option. Reading stories about individuals who have faced trials and come out stronger—like Moses, Abraham, and Job—can be both inspiring and instructive. These stories are a reminder that you are part of a larger plan and that your struggles shape you into who you are meant to be. Reflecting on passages that resonate with your current experiences can be like getting a pat on the back from a wise elder saying, "You've got this!"

Now, let's discuss developing resilience by trusting in God amid life's difficulties. Life is essentially an unending baseball game, so it's inevitable that curveballs are going to keep coming your way. But remember what we spoke about in Chapter 2: Being resilient doesn't mean you'll never fall down; it means you'll bounce back each time you do. Similarly, trusting in God doesn't mean you won't strike out once or twice; it means you're ready to get back to bat, knowing He's cheering you on from the stands.

Making a Difference

We've each been given unique gifts that are just waiting to be unleashed for an extraordinary purpose. Recognizing these talents can often feel like finding hidden treasure within ourselves. Whether it's a knack for making people laugh, a love of music, or a talent for organizing groups, every gift counts. Your job is to understand how you can use these qualities for the greater good.

Think about the incredible diversity of people you cross paths with in your daily life. Everyone has their own strengths and abilities, and when used effectively, they contribute to something far larger than any single person could achieve. Just as Paul mentions in

Romans 12:6, "We have different gifts, according to the grace given to each of us. If your gift is prophesying, then prophesy in accordance with your faith" (*NIV*, 2011/1978). This is a call to action, encouraging you to put your talents to work, not just for your own benefit but to glorify God and serve others.

The next step is to actively take part in community service and volunteer efforts, kind of like what we spoke about earlier. Although volunteering is about helping others, it's also about building connections, learning from those around you, and discovering new ways to apply your God-given talents. Plus, it feels pretty awesome to know you're making a difference.

When you head off on these service opportunities, keeping a few things in mind can make the experience even more rewarding. Start by choosing activities that match your interests and strengths. If you love sports, coaching a local youth team might be your calling. If you're great at art, consider teaching workshops at a community center. The possibilities are endless, and so are the ways you can let your light shine.

Being a Good Influence-r

Being a positive role model is another powerful way to live out your faith. This doesn't mean you have to be perfect—far from it. It means striving to be the best version of yourself and showing kindness, respect, and integrity in everything you do. When others see you consistently practicing what you preach, it inspires them to do the same. And remember, actions often speak louder than words. Sometimes, the most profound impact you can have on someone else's life comes from simply living out your values authentically.

With all the influencers out there doing wild things, it can be pretty motivational for others to see kids their own age who embody these traits. This brings us to the importance of setting a strong example for younger generations. Young people are like sponges, soaking up everything they see and hear. I mean, we all remember the Tide Pod challenge on TikTok, right? By being a role model, you demonstrate that it's possible to stay true to your values while surviving the crazy jungle of modern life.

Here are some practical ways to encourage others by letting your actions speak:

- Engage openly with those around you.
- Share stories of how your faith guides you through challenges.
- Participate in discussions, whether in virtual spaces or in-person gatherings, that allow you to express your beliefs naturally.

It's essential to balance boldness with humility, though, so ensure that your eagerness to share doesn't overshadow your desire to listen and learn from others. This approach builds trust and respect, allowing your actions to plant seeds of curiosity and growth in those around you.

Balancing Boldness and Humility

Speaking of boldness and humility, another important aspect of guiding others is knowing when to discuss your faith openly and when to let your actions do the talking. There are moments when verbal expressions of your beliefs are appropriate and impactful, but there are also times when living out your convictions through quiet strength and gentle influence can be equally powerful. Trust your instincts and pray for guidance to figure out which approach to take in different situations. By doing this, you'll avoid overwhelming others and instead draw them closer to the light you're trying to spread.

We're called to stand firm in our beliefs without becoming self-righteous. That's why it's so important to show respect for differing opinions while staying true to your own. This balance allows you to remain approachable and understanding, which, in turn, opens doors for meaningful conversations and deeper connections.

———

JOURNALING EXERCISE
DEAR FUTURE ME

"'For I know the plans I have for you,' declares the Lord, 'plans to prosper you and not to harm you, plans to give you hope and a future'" (NIV, 2011/1978, Jeremiah 29:11). This verse speaks to God's ongoing work in our lives. It's perfect for this exercise, as it encourages reflection on personal growth in faith.

As we wrap up this section on living out your faith, it's time to look ahead. I want you to take a moment to imagine yourself a year from now, having put into practice the principles we've discussed. Write a letter to your future self addressing the following:

01

Describe how you hope to have grown in your faith over the year.

02

List three specific ways you want to have made a positive impact and served as a light in the world.

03

Share any fears or challenges you anticipate in living out your faith and how you plan to overcome them.

04

Write an encouraging message to your future self, reminding them of God's love and faithfulness.

This exercise will help you set intentions for your spiritual growth and give you a benchmark to measure your progress. It's a reminder that living out your faith is a journey, not a destination, and it's a powerful way to close this chapter and prepare for the next section of this book, "Finding Your Position on God's Team."

JOURNALING EXERCISE
DEAR FUTURE ME

Dear Future Me,

With Love, Future You

Remind me   Send Now

LET'S BRING IT IN

Living out your faith is a bit like being the star in your own Marvel movie, without the cape and supervillains. Throughout this chapter, you've discovered how to take your beliefs from theory to reality—turning them into everyday actions that speak louder than words. From lending a helping hand to standing firm in the face of peer pressure, each small act counts. You've seen that it's not about waiting for a giant spotlight moment but rather embracing those seemingly tiny opportunities to shine God's love brightly. When you do that, you not only make someone else's day a little lighter, but you also grow in your relationship with God.

Now, these strategies might not give you actual superpowers. (Wouldn't that be pretty lit, though?) But they do equip you with something just as powerful: the ability to impact the world around you positively. Whether you're organizing a local charity event or simply sticking up for a friend, every action adds to your personal legacy of faith. So, keep those sneakers tied, your eyes open, and your heart ready—because this is one epic adventure you don't want to miss!

As you move forward, remember that God is with you every step of the way, guiding you and empowering you to be His light in the world. Your experiences of living out your faith will shape your understanding of your unique role in His plan, which we'll really get into in the next section. By actively applying your faith in daily life, you're already playing an essential part on God's team. Let's carry those good vibes into the Second Quarter, where we'll dive deeper into discovering your specific gifts and calling within God's grand game plan.

THE FIRST QUARTER PRAYER

IDENTITY IN CHRIST

Dear God, help me understand who I really am in You.
In Ephesians 2:10, your word says, "For we are God's handiwork,
created in Christ Jesus to do good works, which God prepared in
advance for us to do" (NIV, 2011/1978). Thank You for creating
me with purpose and intention. Give me the wisdom to see
myself through Your eyes, not the world's. Empower me to
embrace the unique way You made me. I'm grateful for Your
perfect design in my life. Help me live each day knowing I'm Your
MVP in Your divine game plan. Let my actions reflect the
confidence of knowing whose team I'm on.
Amen.

PART TWO
FINDING YOUR POSITION ON GOD'S TEAM

THE SECOND QUARTER

FINDING YOUR POSITION ON GOD'S TEAM

For we are God's handiwork,
created in Christ Jesus to do good works,
which God prepared in advance for us to do.
– Ephesians 2:10

CHAPTER 5
DISCOVERING YOUR SPIRITUAL GIFTS: WHAT'S YOUR SUPERPOWER?

God has given you a gift.
The question is, how are you going to use it?
–Joel Osteen

SPOILER ALERT: You've got superpowers! But unlike telekinesis and flying (although that would be cool), these powers are spiritual gifts that make you, well, *you*. Forget about X-ray vision or mind reading; we're talking about abilities like empathy, creativity, leadership, and wisdom—real game-changers that can truly level up your world and the people around you. You could even think of them as jewels tucked away inside you, just waiting to be discovered and polished until they shine their brightest.

But remember that scene in *Spider-Man* where Peter Parker is standing on the roof, trying to figure out how to make his web work? Yeah, that's basically you right now. See, as exciting as it would be to become the next member of the Avengers, this is more about forming deeper connections with others by understanding and nurturing what's already within you.

Now, what does this chapter have in store for our new superhero in training? Get ready to dive into the exciting process of learning how to use your gifts. Once you recognize your standout qualities, you'll realize that they're more than just quirky traits; they're divine tools made specifically for you. We'll also tackle some fun methods to identify these powers—from reflection to taking quizzes and getting feedback from the wise mentors in your life. So, welcome to the journey of self-discovery, where each realization is like a clue on a treasure map leading to a more connected and fulfilling life.

Recognizing Your Spiritual Gifts

Discovering your spiritual gifts is like opening a treasure chest where each gem is a part of who you are meant to be, in both the cosmic sense and here on Earth among your homies and the fam. Sure, you might not get a cape or the ability to fly, but these gifts are even more special: They're the talents that make up the essence of who you are. And it's the same for everybody. Understanding that everyone has distinct talents is a great starting point. We've all got unique sparkles that define us—it's as though we're all walking kaleidoscopes.

These aren't just cool abilities like being able to juggle five oranges or do an epic skateboard trick. They are those deep-seated qualities that speak to your soul's purpose. Whether it's empathy, leadership, creativity, or wisdom, these gifts form an integral part of who you are. They are like a cool secret handshake between the universe and you, setting you apart in a magnificent way.

Now, you might wonder, *Why should I care about these gifts?* Well, recognizing them helps in shaping your identity. Imagine trying to build a LEGO model without knowing what it is. You'd end up with random pieces scattered everywhere! In the same way, without acknowledging your spiritual gifts, your identity can feel like it's all over the show. It's these qualities that add vibrancy to your character and determine how you fit into the larger puzzle of your community.

When you embrace them, you can see yourself more clearly, and others will also start to see your unique attributes, turning regular convos into meaningful connections. This is true for a whole different bunch of contributions, from jokes that leave people holding onto their sides to insightful thoughts that really hit people deep in the feels.

Life Hacks for Uncovering Your Hidden Gifts
So, how do we pinpoint these spiritual goodies?

Reflection
Method number one: reflection. Sounds simple, right? Taking time to think about what activities or situations make you feel most alive, purposeful, or joyful can point you toward your hidden gifts. It's like being on a scavenger hunt where clues unfold the path to your treasure chest. You might find that journaling or meditation can lead to revelations about your personal strengths and passions.

After all, sometimes, the gift is in seeing the world through your own quirky lens.

Assessments

The second method involves assessments. Quizzes aren't just for school—they're also great tools for self-discovery. There are lots of different assessments out there that can help you find potential areas of strength. The aim of taking them isn't to label yourself but to shine a spotlight on any hidden abilities that you may otherwise miss in the daily grind. Consider it the magical Sorting Hat of spiritual gifts; while these tests don't label you permanently, they do give you an initial nudge in the right direction.

Feedback

Then, there's feedback from mentors or your parents. Trusted adults serve as mirrors reflecting back our genuine selves, sometimes clearer than we can see ourselves. These wise sages of your personal journey can provide insights that you might overlook. Sometimes, they recognize things in you that you take for granted because those traits are just second nature to you.

Let's say, for example, a mentor tells you that you have the incredible gift of patience. At first, you might shrug it off, thinking, *I'm just chill*. However, the more you think about it, the more you see that you often help friends through tough times and make chaotic situations seem manageable. This realization doesn't just enhance your appreciation for this gift but encourages you to start using it in different situations.

Incorporating feedback requires you to be open and humble, but it enriches the journey of appreciating your gifts. This guidance is like getting a friendly map that points out hidden trails you've overlooked along the path of life. It might even feel a bit like having a personal tour guide helping you navigate what makes you distinctly you and encouraging you to channel it for good.

Discovering and appreciating your spiritual gifts isn't about being better than anyone else, though. Rather, when more of us become aware of our God-given strengths, we can form an all-star team where everyone brings something valuable to the table. Each gift contributes uniquely to the community, turning it into a place where diversity becomes strength.

Recognizing and building a positive self-identity based on these God-given strengths helps you create a more confident version of yourself. With clarity about your gifts, facing up to challenges becomes more like playing your favorite video game but with cheat codes that boost your self-awareness and connection with others.

Developing and Enhancing Spiritual Gifts

We've touched on how spiritual gifts are all about making the world a better place, so let's dive into how you can hone the powers you've uncovered and turn them up to 11.

Time and Place

First things first: finding the right setting. Just like Batman needs his lair, you need an environment that nurtures your spiritual growth. Think about where you feel most connected. Is it in nature? At a buzzing community center? Or is it maybe in the peace of your room, with a good playlist on in the background? It's all about finding a zone you can vibe in, a place where your mind can chill and think deep thoughts. This is the fertile ground where your gifts will start to grow.

Strategy

Now, let's talk strategy. Because having powers is cool, but knowing how to use them is epic. Practice makes perfect—even Spider-Man had to learn how to swing without smacking into walls. Start with small actions that echo your spiritual gift, like organizing an event if leadership is your thing or volunteering at a local shelter if giving back is more your vibe. The secret sauce is practice combined with patience. Over time, these small steps will boost your confidence and level up your abilities in ways you never imagined possible. And remember, even the best heroes have mentors, so don't be shy to seek guidance and feedback from people you trust.

Collaboration

Speaking of collaboration, when gifted individuals unite, magic happens. (Think more Justice League than Suicide Squad.) Combining your gifts with those of others doesn't just multiply the impact—it takes it from 0 to 100 real quick. For example, if you're awesome at storytelling, link up with someone who's a natural at coding. Together, you could create a platform where other teens can share their stories and build an online community of support and inspiration. It's like assembling your own Avengers team, minus the bickering over who gets to be Iron Man.

Using Your Spiritual Gifts for Service

Your talents are here to transform the world around you and make it a better place. Think of them as secret weapons that you can use to serve others, like how Luke Cage and Daredevil use their powers to fight crime.

Flexing Your Gifts

First off, let's get one thing straight—spiritual gifts are about way more than self-improvement and personal glory. Sure, they help us grow, but their real magic kicks in when we use them for the greater good. It's like everyone in your community holds a part of an enormous puzzle. You've got a piece, and it's unique to you. Without it, that puzzle won't ever be complete. Using your gifts to help others fits your piece into that grand design, creating something amazing.

So, where can you flex these super-gifts? Look around! Community centers, youth groups, and local charities are awesome places to start. You might be great at organizing fundraisers, counseling friends, or even whipping up some legendary cookies for a bake sale. All of these talents can have a surprisingly large impact. You just need to look for areas where you can jump in and make a difference.

Gifts of the Spirit

Now, if you're wondering what God has to do with all this, just hear me out. Scripture gives some solid advice about these strengths. It's like a manual for using your powers wisely. According to 1 Corinthians 12, we've all been given different gifts by the Spirit. The words of this passage might sound ancient, but the idea is timeless: We're all parts of one big body. We need each other.

Your ability to play the guitar or crack jokes could be just as important as someone else's knack for public speaking. And every time you use your gift, you're being an agent of God's grace, like it says in Corinthians. Don't let your talents gather dust; bring them out into the open and let them shine.

Hometown Heroes

Just in case you think this is all talk and no action, let's look at some real-life heroes who've used their gifts well. Take Jamie, for example. He was just a regular kid who loved fiddling with computers. But when his church faced tech issues, he stepped in, volunteering his skills. It wasn't long before he was connecting the whole community by helping folks who couldn't attend in person stream services. Another case? Meet my girl Lisa. She took her knack for storytelling and turned it into a mission trip blog that raised awareness and funds for her cause. These examples prove that using your gifts can lead to epic outcomes.

Feeling inspired? Great! Now, how do you go from discovering your gifts to actually using them? A little brainstorming session can work wonders. Scribble down some activities you enjoy, whether it's painting, mentoring, or budgeting, and see how they can fit into community service. If you're still unsure, chat with a mentor or trusted adult who knows your strengths; they might see angles you haven't considered.

Keep Going, Keep Growing

Everyone's journey with their spiritual gifts is different. One person's path may involve leading worship, while another's could be shaped by quietly working behind the scenes. The important thing is to keep exploring and never stop learning. Having a spiritual gift is only the starting point; it can only serve its purpose if you develop it over time and see where it leads you.

As you use your talents in the service of others, you'll notice something incredible happening: growth. Just like muscles strengthen with exercise, your spiritual gifts will expand and evolve. You'll find yourself more attuned to opportunities and more effective in your service. Before you know it, you'll be making waves not just in your own life but in the lives of those around you.

———

🕴 EQ EXERCISE: GIFT DETECTOR

In 1 Corinthians 12:4, when Paul says, "There are different kinds of gifts, but the same Spirit distributes them," his emphasis on the diversity of spiritual gifts encourages us to appreciate our unique abilities (NIV, 2011/1978). This forms the basis of our next exercise.

For the next week, I want you to pay attention to activities that really hype you up and situations where you feel like you're in your main character energy. These could be clues to your spiritual gifts. You can take your reflection even further by writing down what you observe and considering why these things excite you.

INTROSPECTIVE JOURNALING
SUPERHERO TEAM-UP

Earlier, we spoke about how your quest isn't just about self-improvement —it's also about using these blossoming skills to do good. So, as you hone your gifts, remember that the ultimate aim is godly service. This sentiment is reflected in 1 Peter 4:10, which mentions, "Each of you should use whatever gift you have received to serve others, as faithful stewards of God's grace in its various forms" (NIV, 2011/1978).

For this next exercise, start by reflecting on these words for a moment and consider what they mean to you. Then, write about how your gifts could complement those of your friends or family members to make a positive impact.

Whether it's helping others find their unique talents or contributing to your community's well-being, you're harnessing a force for the greater good. So, suit up, embrace these tasks, and watch your influence ripple outward.

LET'S BRING IT IN

In this chapter of our spiritual journey, we've ventured into the realm of personal superpowers—those unique spiritual gifts that set you apart and make the world light up with possibility. You've learned how these gifts form a core part of your identity and are your cosmic high-five from the universe. By embracing them, you add an epic piece to the puzzle of your community, leveling up your connections and brightening your place in the masterpiece of life. Through reflection, assessments, or seeking feedback from wise mentors, uncovering these treasures within can lead to adventures bigger than the plot of any blockbuster movie you've ever seen. Yes, even End Game and Infinity War.

Now, you're ready to unleash these amazing abilities for something even more extraordinary. From organizing events to cracking jokes or volunteering, there's a world of opportunities waiting for your unique contributions. You hold a magical key that unlocks doors to serving others. Whether it's building community bonds or making someone smile when they need it most, you can sprinkle positivity into every day. So, ignite those hidden talents, link up with other gifted heroes, and watch as you transform your surroundings and impact lives in ways that only you can.

CHAPTER 6
DRAFT DAY – SHOWING UP ON THE LORD'S TEAM

We have different gifts,
according to the grace given to each of us.
–Romans 12:6

IMAGINE JUST WAKING up one day and being told that you've been handpicked to play in God's ultimate match. No pressure, right? Forget about those school games; this is a whole different ballpark! But like any good coach would say, it all starts with understanding your motivations. You could compare it to choosing between two pairs of kicks. On the one hand, you have a flashy, fancy set of sneakers that look great but give you blisters. On the other, you have some sturdy, reliable cleats that won't let you down halfway through the game. The first option might draw attention, but the second helps you score the winning goal. It's about making smart plays with divine guidance.

In this chapter, we're not just warming up or stretching—we're figuring out how to be MVPs on God's squad. To start, you'll reflect on whether you're chasing after temporary glory or aiming for something eternal. You'll also learn why internal motivations are more than just another pep talk and see why they're literally a game-changer. Later, we'll explore some amazing stories and strategies that'll help you figure out your role in this divine game plan. From drafting biblical all-stars like Joseph and Moses to challenging you to align your daily goals with spiritual intentions, this chapter's got you covered with everything you need to learn how to turn everyday actions into methods of serving a greater purpose. So, suit up; it's time to hit the field and see what being on the Lord's team truly means.

Discovering Diverse Motivations

Considering the various motivations that drive you is kind of like building a sundae at an ice cream shop. You've got internal motivations, which are basically your hot fudge sauce—stuff like passion, curiosity, and a genuine love for what you're doing. Then, there's the external stuff, like getting good grades or winning awards—these are more like those extra cherries on top. They're nice, but they're not the core of your dessert.

Why Motivation Matters

Now, let's dig into why motivation matters when it comes to understanding how we align with God's game plan.

Internal Motivations

First, there are internal motivations. These are the passions and interests that really get you hyped; they are essential because they often reveal your God-given talents. But how do you know if these are aligned with God's plans? Well, that's where prayer and reflection come in handy—it's like asking for directions when you're a bit lost. Allowing God to lead the way means using your unique design to bring Him glory and serving others while you're at it.

External Motivations

Then, there's the matter of external motivations. While it's cool to get props or applause, these shouldn't be the main focus of your life's purpose. Growth happens when you focus on what God wants instead of chasing clout. So, simply put, your passions should ideally contribute to something bigger than yourself.

Aligning with divine intent means turning prayers into productive action, making the steps you take toward your goals as important as the prayers themselves. When you hit the balance, you'll do things for personal satisfaction and let your actions speak for your faith.

Biblical MVPs Who Deserve a Shoutout

Let's flip through the Bible for some role models. Joseph's story is a touchdown example. Can you just imagine what it would be like being sold into slavery by your brothers and facing cultural hurdles yet still staying true to God? That isn't just dedication; it's MVP-level persistence. Despite his circumstances, Joseph stayed committed to God's plan, and bam! He eventually became Egypt's go-to guy during the famine.

Moses adds another impressive chapter to the Biblical Hall of Fame. Although he grew up in the Pharaoh's crib, he felt the tug of his Hebrew roots, so he had dual motivations kicking in. The

Egyptian palace life was no doubt comfy, but he strapped up his sandals and took on the mission to free his peeps anyway. Talk about hard decisions and divine focus.

Get the Lowdown on Your Motivations

So, how do you convert your daily hustle into fulfilling God's ultimate plan?

- First, you've got to understand your motivations deeply. Take some time to reflect: find a quiet spot, grab a journal, and let your thoughts fly. Ask yourself why you pursue certain goals. Is it hopes for fame and fortune, or is it something deeper? If it's the latter, you might be on the right track.
- Consider how your actions serve others and glorify God. Volunteering, mentoring, or simply being a good friend can reflect divine purpose. The idea is that your behavior should echo what Jesus emphasized—love, compassion, and connection.

Let's wrap this section up with some practical steps that you can treat as guidelines to help you along the way:

- One method is setting mini goals that align with your bigger purpose. Trust me, nothing feels better than going through your to-do list and checking boxes that contribute to the greater good.
- Also, surround yourself with people who support you in this quest for divine fulfillment. They're the cheerleaders on your sidelines, reminding you of your purpose even when you doubt it.

And remember, when you take delight in God, you'll see how desires start aligning.

Embracing Integrity and Authenticity

In the game plan of life, integrity guides every move. It's like the coach of your basketball team laying out the strategy for winning. If you don't follow it, there'll be absolute chaos. Similarly, on the divine field, integrity is what helps us make sure that we reflect God's presence in our daily plays.

Why Integrity Matters

But what exactly is integrity, and why should you care about it? I'm so glad you asked!

Having integrity means being honest and reliable; it means having strong moral principles, even when nobody's watching. It's doing the right thing just because it's the right thing to do, not because you expect a reward or fear punishment. Essentially, integrity is about authenticity. You could say that it's not just about playing the game but playing it right.

In biblical terms, it means embodying sincerity, trustworthiness, and truthfulness. God values these traits deeply; we know this because they can be found all over Scripture, guiding how we worship and live our lives. For instance, John 4:23–24 (*NIV*, 2011/1978) tells us the following:

Yet a time is coming and has now come when the true worshipers will worship the Father in the Spirit and in truth, for they are the kind of worshipers the Father seeks. God is spirit, and his worshipers must worship in the Spirit and in truth.

You Are a Temple

Now, let's dive into the idea of being God's temple. No, this doesn't mean you suddenly identify as a building. Instead, it's about recognizing that God's spirit lives within you, making your actions and decisions vital reflections of His character. Just imagine yourself as a glowing lighthouse in the middle of a stormy sea. When you embrace your role as a home for the Holy Spirit, others see that light, feel its warmth, and can find their own paths better. It's the ultimate teamwork—your integrity inspires others to strengthen theirs. Wherever you go, whether it's school, the sports field, or chilling with the boys, remember that you carry this incredible responsibility to let His light shine through you.

Keeping It 100

So, how do you maintain your integrity in everyday life? Well, life throws all kinds of crazy opportunities your way. Often, they will test your ethics, like when someone asks you to help them cheat on a test or when you consider pocketing a few extra dollars from your part-time job. We've all faced those tiny, seemingly harmless temptations. But living with integrity means choosing honesty even when the stakes appear low. Simple practices, like speaking the truth, owning up to mistakes, and treating others fairly, become testimonies of your faith. Ultimately, integrity aligns your behaviors with your beliefs, ensuring your outward actions match your inward commitment to God's ways.

Home Base

Your community also plays a pretty big role in supporting your drive toward authenticity. Think of it as your home base in the game of life: This is a place full of people who always have your back and teammates who are cheering you on, ready to pass the ball when you need help. In essence, your community strengthens your determination to live with integrity, and they give you plenty of guidance and companionship along the way.

In church or youth groups, you and like-minded friends can hold each other accountable. These people remind you to stay true to your commitments, celebrate successes, and learn from setbacks. They can offer you advice and encouragement, and their support is like a buffer when you fumble.

Living a life of integrity sometimes means you gotta put certain virtues above loyalty to institutions. Regardless of external pressures, staying true to God's teachings means keeping the balance between loving Him and loving your neighbors. Balance is what makes sure that you act justly, love mercy, and walk humbly before the Lord.

Aligning Your Goals With God's Will

Let's face it—sometimes our personal goals feel like LEGO pieces tossed across the floor. You might have a vision for what you want, but actually putting those pieces together in a way that serves God can be kinda rough. It may feel like you're building something entirely off-track. But you know what? Aligning your personal goals with God's purpose is just as rewarding as nailing the perfect game-winning play.

Making Sure You're on the Right Track

When it comes to aligning your motivations with your divine purpose, one of the most important steps involves a bit of self-reflection. That's why the first maneuver in this divine playbook is understanding what your current goals are and how they align—or don't—with God's bigger plans.

Regularly checking in with yourself helps you to ensure that your goals resonate with God's desires for you. Take some time to list your current aspirations on paper—improved grades, stronger friendships, better athletic performance—and examine whether they align with your spiritual values. Then, ask if these goals support your spiritual growth or serve others as God intended. Ask yourself, *Is this designed by me, or does it reflect God's game plan? Are these goals promoting personal growth and kindness?* If so, great! If not, it might be time to make a few changes.

This exercise isn't about beating yourself up but understanding the motivations behind your actions. When your intentions clash with integrity, it's like trying to score a goal at the wrong end of the field. However, by honestly assessing your aims, you can correct and redirect your energy toward things that are more meaningful.

When you have misaligned goals, it's like you're in a football game but running plays from a different sport altogether. However, rather than giving up, you can learn how to steer those goals onto God's field. For instance, maybe you've been working around the clock to get into a top college just for the prestige. Sure, being accepted to an Ivy League school is admirable, but does it align with God's purpose for you? Redirect that goal to serve God by thinking about how attending college can help you gain skills to better serve your community or address other issues important to God. This might mean choosing a field of study focused on helping others or maybe using campus resources to start a faith-based student group.

Of course, when you focus on God's game plan, Scripture is your go-to guide. The Bible provides plenty of verses that encourage you to make sure everything you do is for the Lord rather than human approval. For example, Colossians 3:23 says, "Whatever you do, work at it with all your heart, as working for the Lord, not for human masters," (*NIV*, 2011/1978). Here, it's pretty clear that our actions should glorify God. Instead of grinding for clout, think about how your work, talent, or achievements bring glory to Him.

In the grand scheme, every goal, aspiration, and dream reflects part of God's story. By aligning your desires with His divine narrative, you become a more authentic part of His team. Remember, God doesn't draft benchwarmers. He handpicks key players and actively shapes their roles on and off the field. Whether through silent acts of kindness or leading large initiatives, each of your actions—big or small—plays an important part in fulfilling His plan.

🕴 *EQ EXERCISE: MOTIVATION CHECK*

Colossians 3:23, which was quoted in the previous section, encourages us to align our motivations with serving God, not just pleasing others. Bearing this in mind, I want you to complete the following exercise:

01

Write down how each of your goals contributes to God's team.

02

Similarly, jot down your dreams and fears.

03

Pull apart each one to see if it fits within God's framework.

This helps you understand and internalize your true priorities and determine if they are aligned with God's purposes.

INTROSPECTIVE JOURNALING
LOCKER ROOM TALK

Hebrews 10:24 states, "And let us consider how we may spur one another on toward love and good deeds" (NIV, 2011/1978). This emphasizes the importance of encouraging each other in our faith.

So, for this exercise, I want you to grab a notebook and write a pep talk to yourself, focusing on your role on God's team and how you can encourage others.

LET'S BRING IT IN

Life's game plan can feel like a never-ending puzzle, but this chapter has offered a playful road map that you can use to guide you along the way. We've dived into the world of motivations, both internal and external, and seen how they're like your favorite ice cream toppings. Whether you're in it for the sprinkles (that sweet passion) or just after cherries on top (external rewards), what really matters is knowing where you stand with God's game plan. You've also seen how cooling down with some self-reflection, journaling, and prayer can help ensure that your moves are part of His larger strategy. Just think of Moses and Joseph—two MVPs who turned their life's plot twists into divine touchdowns because they trusted the playbook Christ handed to them.

Now, before you rush off to tackle life like a football game, remember the power of integrity and authenticity. This isn't about being Mr. Perfect; nah fam, it's about embracing honesty and reliability even when no one's looking. Living by these values makes you a lighthouse for others, guiding them through life's stormy seas. And don't forget—your community is your hype squad, supporting you as you align your daily actions with divine intent. By doing this, you're living out a story much larger than yourself.

This chapter has shown that stepping up as a key player involves more than scoring points—it's about aligning your goals with God's will and living each day with humor, heart, and purpose. You're now officially part of the greatest team in history, one where every player is important. God has drafted you for a reason, so get out there and play your heart out for Him!

CHAPTER 7
LEVEL UP YOUR STRENGTHS AND SKILLS

Each of you should use whatever gift you have received
to serve others, as faithful stewards of God's grace
in its various forms.
–1 Peter 4:10

LEVELING up your strengths and skills is like gearing up in a video game, but instead of cool armor and epic weapons, you're arming yourself with abilities that can lead to real-life victories. In this chapter, we'll take what you learned about your spiritual superpowers in the previous chapters and take it even further, showing you how you can improve what you're naturally good at. Whether it's dribbling a soccer ball like Messi or being the friend everyone turns to for advice, these strengths make you stand out in your unique way. So, get ready to explore how acknowledging and building on these natural abilities can transform your everyday life from ordinary to extraordinary.

As with any quest, there's more to the journey than flexing your talents. This chapter will also guide you through understanding weaknesses, encouraging you to see them not as downfalls but as areas ripe for improvement. Then, we'll walk through spotting opportunities. These real-life side quests might involve joining a club or taking on exciting projects; whatever form they take, it's up to you to accept them. Threats, those pesky obstacles that lurk like your ex on your social media posts, are out there, too. But don't worry, I'm not leaving you defenseless. Nah, fam, I've got your back. I'm about to hook you up with strategies you can use to tackle challenges head-on.

From helping you harness your God-given talents to walking you through how to leap over those hurdles, this chapter will be your trusty guidebook, paving the way for personal growth and improved effectiveness. Are you ready to head off on a mission where you not only play the game but become the hero of your own story? Grab your controller—or rather, your journal—and let's start leveling up!

SWOT Analysis for Personal Growth

When you're fixing to head out on the quest to level up your strengths and skills, one essential tool you can wield is the SWOT analysis. Originally designed for businesses, this analytical framework can help you evaluate and enhance your personal growth as an individual. But don't let the fancy acronym intimidate you; SWOT just stands for

- strengths
- weaknesses

- opportunities
- threats

It's a failsafe gadget that's there to shed light on the paths ahead and the pits to avoid.

Evaluating Your Strengths

Your strengths are your natural abilities, the things you're just effortlessly good at—and that's pretty lit, right? Whether you're a whiz at science, a budding artist, or a comedic genius with the enviable skill of making people laugh until they cry, these talents contribute positively to your personal and even spiritual life. Remember what I said in Chapter 5: They're like superpowers that have been gifted to you, and acknowledging them is the first step to harnessing their full potential.

Think about what you identified in the previous exercises and anything else that makes you stand out in a crowd. Then, reflect on how you can use these attributes to amplify your journey of self-discovery and development.

Recognizing Your Weaknesses

Now, onto the not-so-glamorous part: weaknesses. Everyone's got 'em, even Batman (he's human, after all), so don't be too afraid to take the L, fam. Recognizing these limitations allows you to identify areas where you might need a bit more backup or practice. Maybe your time management needs some work, or maybe public speaking makes your knees wobble.

Shining a light on these areas doesn't mean you're doomed—it means you've found places to improve. And that's great because growth is why we're here, isn't it? Weaknesses are just opportunities in disguise, offering you the chance to expand and evolve.

Finding Opportunities

Speaking of opportunities, let's switch it up and talk about those. This is where the real adventure begins. Opportunities are VIP passes; they're chances to put your skills into action and maybe even discover new ones along the way. Whether it's joining a club at school, volunteering, or taking on a challenging project, there are options everywhere—you've just got to keep your eyes peeled.

Ask yourself, *How can I use my current strengths?* If you're a creative writer, could you submit a piece to the school magazine? If you're a tech enthusiast, could you help with sound and lighting for a community event? With each opportunity seized, you get closer to refining your talents and discovering new avenues for success.

Identifying Threats

But hold up—before you rush off into the horizon, watch your back for those potential threats. No, not actual monsters, but the obstacles that might derail your progress. Think of these as quicksand patches on your journey. They could be external pressures like societal expectations or internal battles in the form of self-doubt and procrastination.

Knowing what threats are hanging over your head is half the battle won. By assessing potential challenges and planning strategies to combat them, you empower yourself with the knowledge to swerve them with swag. For example, you could set small, achievable goals to build confidence or hit up a friend and ask them to be your motivational buddy to tackle procrastination.

Ultimately, the beauty of conducting a SWOT analysis is that it gives you clarity. It helps map out both smooth roads and bumpy trails, allowing you to strategize effectively. When it comes to your personal development, understanding these elements paves the way to becoming a well-rounded individual who fully connects with their unique gifts while tackling weaknesses head-on.

Strategies for Developing and Applying Your Strengths

When you're leveling up your strengths and skills, establishing a solid action plan is a must. Think of it like being the director of your own movie, where you decide how each scene plays out. You already took the first step (identifying what you rock at) when you completed your SWOT analysis. Now, you can figure out how to go even further by developing a personalized action plan that highlights these talents.

After pinpointing specific strengths that you want to work on, like refining your wicked sense of humor or turning your gaming strategy skills into leadership abilities, list down clear goals. For example, writing a joke every day or organizing a tournament among friends. This way, you're not just imagining improvement; you're taking concrete steps to make it happen.

But hold on, this isn't a one-time project you cram into one night; it's more like training for a marathon. Just like in video games, you need to hit those XP points daily if you want to reach the next level. Regular practice routines are your secret weapons here. Maybe it's setting aside time each week to write, draw, or practice coding. If you keep at it, over time, you'll notice your skills level up. Consistency is key, my friend.

Don't forget about the power of mentorship and resources. Everyone benefits from a guide or mentor who's been there and done that. Whether it's asking a teacher for guidance in science or joining a local club with people who share your interests, these connections can propel you forward faster than if you go solo. Consider online courses or YouTube tutorials, too; they're modern-day spellbooks filled with knowledge.

Of course, measuring and reviewing progress is crucial. Just as gamers track their high scores or athletes note their times, keeping tabs on your development is essential. Create a habit of checking in with yourself. Set small milestones and celebrate when you hit them. Maybe after a month of practicing guitar, you can finally play that tricky song. Celebrate it! Reflect on what worked and what didn't, then adjust your plans accordingly.

A positive mindset is like wearing the ultimate suit of armor—it makes you invincible. It's recognizing that you're wonderfully made and that you have a bunch of special traits tucked away inside you. When you focus on the good stuff and celebrate the strengths God has given you, it opens up a whole new world of possibilities. You'll notice the little things that make you shine and start seeing the bright side, even in tough situations.

———

⚭ INTROSPECTIVE JOURNALING
PERSONAL SWOT ANALYSIS

In the Bible, 2 Corinthians 13:5 encourages self-reflection and evaluation. This verse states, "Examine yourselves to see whether you are in the faith; test yourselves" (NIV, 2011/1978). With that in mind, I want you to conduct a personal SWOT analysis of your spiritual life and character.

Asking yourself some simple questions can open doors to deeper understanding. Here are some good examples:

01

What strengths do you possess that give you an edge in school projects?

02

What weaknesses might slow you down while pursuing hobbies?

03

How can you be more proactive about taking opportunities that align your actions with growth?

04

What strategies can you devise to handle your threats effectively?

A personal SWOT analysis shines a light on areas in need of focus and reveals paths you likely hadn't considered, but it's not a one-time activity. By doing this regularly, you'll be able to maintain a keen awareness of your evolving story and gain insights into creating future chapters.

INTROSPECTIVE JOURNALING
PERSONAL SWOT ANALYSIS

01

What strengths do
you possess that
give you an edge in
school projects?

INTROSPECTIVE JOURNALING
PERSONAL SWOT ANALYSIS

02

What weaknesses might
slow you down while
pursuing hobbies?

03

How can you be more proactive about taking opportunities that align your actions with growth?

INTROSPECTIVE JOURNALING
PERSONAL SWOT ANALYSIS

04

What strategies can
you devise to handle
your threats
effectively?

MINDSET PRACTICE
STRENGTH SPOTTER

Psalm 139:14, which states, "I praise you because I am fearfully and wonderfully made; your works are wonderful, I know that full well" (NIV, 2011/1978), reminds us that our strengths are part of God's wonderful design. To really drive this home, I want you to do the following exercise:

> Each day for a week, pick one cool trait you've noticed in yourself and in someone else. Maybe you're super patient, or perhaps your friend is a wizard at telling a story. Jot these down in your journal. Not only does it give you warm fuzzy feelings about yourself and others, but it also helps you appreciate all the unique abilities people have.

Having a diverse crew means that you'll identify loads of different abilities and perspectives. Appreciating those unique qualities in others and using that understanding allows you to create connections. When you develop a knack for spotting strengths in your friends or family, you're building empathy. And guess what? This newfound skill can help you communicate better and build rock-solid relationships.

LET'S BRING IT IN

As we wrap up this chapter, let's take a moment to look back on our quest for personal growth and superhero-level skills. We've explored the mighty SWOT analysis—a secret tool hiding in plain sight. This little acronym might sound like a character from a sci-fi flick, but it's more like your personal assistant, helping you map out your strengths, face those pesky weaknesses, seize golden opportunities, and swerve potential threats quicker than you can say "Oops!"

Whether you're a natural-born comedian, a tech whiz, or just have a knack for making pizzas disappear, recognizing your strengths is like finding out you're the main character in your own cool movie. But every hero has their challenges. (Kryptonite, anyone?) Maybe procrastination feels like your uninvited sidekick, or perhaps public speaking makes you feel as unstable as a Jenga tower. That's okay! We've all got weaknesses, and that's what makes us human. The trick is knowing where you can level up. So, why not pick up that journal and start jotting down those epic victories, daring quests, and maybe even a doodle or two of your future self owning it?

And as a bonus, remember to sprinkle some empathy around and appreciate the strengths in others, too—it's like adding extra lives to your game. Leveling up is a continuous process, but with God's help, you're well on your way to becoming the ultimate player He designed you to be. Keep up with these practices and watch as you evolve into the champion of your story, ready to tackle any challenge with a smile and an arsenal of super skills.

CHAPTER 8
FLEX THOSE SPIRITUAL MUSCLES: PUTTING YOUR STRENGTHS TO WORK

Your talent is God's gift to you.
What you do with it is your gift back to God.
–Leo Buscaglia

LIKE SUPERMAN'S suit that's always hidden beneath Clark Kent's clothes, you've got strengths just waiting to burst out and make an impact on the world around you. Imagine if you could use those unique abilities to change how you vibe with people, deal with drama, or even influence your community. That's what this chapter is here to help you accomplish. It's about equipping you to recognize the gifts you've been given from above and showing you how to unleash them in ways that transform ordinary days into meaningful adventures.

We'll start off by exploring what it means to commit to your faith on a personal level and how that commitment can affect all areas of your life. Then, we'll discuss how relationships don't just thrive on love or kindness alone. They need the spice of empathy, active listening, and open communication to turn mundane moments into epic memories. So, you'll discover life hacks for applying these strengths in your relationships to make them livelier and more authentic.

We'll also unpack the idea of using your talents for positive social impact. Whether it's volunteering at local shelters, starting your own community projects, or assembling a team to clean up the neighborhood, putting your skills to work can inspire waves of change. By the end of this chapter, you'll see how each choice you make—big or small—is an opportunity to flex your spiritual muscles and create a legacy of goodness. And, I mean, who wouldn't want that, right?

Making a Personal Commitment to Faith

Flexing spiritual muscles isn't just for religious heavyweights; you can do it, too. You just need to figure out how making a personal faith commitment can really shake up your everyday moves. But we're taking it a step further: The goal here is to understand not just what you've got inside you but how trusting in something bigger can send ripples through each day.

Recognizing Your Talents as Divine Gifts

First things first, let's talk about talents. At this point, you know that you have them, even if you still think that juggling oranges or solving a Rubik's Cube at lightning speed doesn't count. But now that you've done the work of identifying them and appreciate them as gifts from God, you need to become intentional about using them.

When you see these talents as divine blessings meant to be used with purpose, every action—like helping someone understand a math problem or creating art—becomes a way of expressing faith. Once you're able to see your skills as divine gifts, you can ensure that your actions make a tangible difference in your surroundings, whether that's within your family, school, or wider community.

Facing Challenges

Now, let's address the elephant in the room. Daily challenges might seem like they're out to get you, but embracing them is like lifting spiritual weights. Each one you confront strengthens your faith muscles. Or, if the gym's not your vibe, think of it like playing a video game where each level gets tougher but also more rewarding once you conquer it. By facing these challenges head-on, you learn resilience, patience, and trust. Just think of those spiritual gains!

Taking Faith to the Streets

Speaking of trust, let's get into consistent acts of kindness and generosity. This is where faith goes public and where your beliefs make a real impact. Whether it's holding the door open for someone or collecting blankets for a local shelter, these acts scream compassion. As much as kindness and generosity are good deeds, they're also reflections of your values put into action. They demonstrate a living faith that isn't shy about being seen or felt.

Keeping Your Eyes on the Prize

Building a routine that includes mindfulness and reflection is like installing an app that helps you stay focused on what really matters. When you incorporate moments of quiet reflection into your daily routine, you create space for gratitude, self-awareness, and spiritual growth. When you set aside time for prayer or meditation, you can reflect on your day and align your thoughts with your values. It gives you a chance to adjust so that your actions are intentional and grounded in faith.

Tying all these points together makes it clear that a personal commitment to faith isn't a one-off event—it's a lifestyle. It shapes how you interact with others, face challenges, and use your talents. The influence of faith on daily life is profound and comes in so many different forms, transforming seemingly ordinary actions into testimonies of belief and purpose. When you commit to your faith, you're essentially deciding to let it color every aspect of your life and guide all your decisions and interactions.

Using Talents to Enhance Relationships

Ever noticed how some family gatherings feel like a comedy show while others are just awkward silence? (I'm cringing just thinking about it.) And have you ever been around friends who can make even a trip to the grocery store a tale for the ages? Here's a secret: The magic often lies in the role empathy, active listening, and good old open communication play in improving our family and social dynamics. Let's see how you can flex these muscles.

Empathy

Let's say your friend just got dumped. Empathy is like putting on their kicks because you're trying to understand what they're going through. When your homie is moping about their tragic love story, it's your understanding nods and open ears that'll support them through the saga. But if empathy isn't naturally your vibe, don't sweat it! According to the HIGH5 test (an online quiz that helps you figure out what your top strengths are; go on and look it up if you're curious), you can still approach it with a twist by focusing on understanding challenges as a problem solver.

Active Listening

Next time your family dinner feels more like a silent film, why not try being an active listener? Giving your attention, in full, is pretty important, even if you'd rather be reading your detective novel or scrolling through your socials under the table. Instead of plotting your daring escape from Uncle Bob's long-winded story-telling, tune in and maybe drop a "Really? Then what happened?" Suddenly, you're not just hearing words; you're picking up on needs and emotions. This attention could mean all the difference between missed connections and deeply felt bonds.

Open Communication

Ah, open communication—a concept as simple as texting a friend yet sometimes as hard as winning at a claw machine. But it's the secret sauce for creating those Hallmark-movie moments in your relationships. Encouraging vulnerability opens the door to honest communication. Letting your guard down is not a sign of weakness; rather, it turns small talk into DMCs. Think of it this way: When you share your triumphs and tragedies with your squad, they receive an invitation to do the same. So, the next time your sibling starts venting about school stress, lower the screen and show genuine interest. Maybe chip in with a bit of your own chaos. It's through this exchange that connection truly grows.

Celebrate Wins

Whether it's someone passing an exam, getting a new job, or just surviving another Monday, it's important to throw mini celebrations. Did your friend nail their economics presentation? Break out that dance move you've been saving or send them a silly meme. Celebrating others' successes doesn't require a red-carpet event. Heartfelt acknowledgment is all it takes to let them know their victory matters to you, too.

Creating a supportive vibe is like growing a garden; it thrives on consistent care and attention. Maybe you can consider throwing surprise recognition parties, launching a "thank you" note attack, or just applauding when someone finally does their laundry. What's important is making others feel seen and valued. These small gestures can help create a sense of belonging and unconditional support within relationships.

Remember to Be Grateful

Practicing gratitude can also work wonders here. Maybe you can start keeping a journal or create a group chat dedicated to sharing daily highlights and things you're grateful for. This habit can shift everyone's focus toward the positive aspects of life and strengthen the bond among family members and friends.

Conflict Resolution

Lastly, let's get down to the nitty-gritty stuff. Conflict resolution may sound intense, but when it's approached with empathy and strong communication, it becomes easier. Patience, understanding, and willingness to find common ground make all the difference. By recognizing others' perspectives and expressing your own calmly, disagreements become stepping stones to stronger and longer-lasting relationships.

Community Glow Up

Dude, have you ever thought about flexing those spiritual muscles of yours in the community? I know it sounds epic, right? Whether you're looking to save the world or just your drama club, using your personal strengths can make a big difference. I mean, if the friendly neighborhood Spider-Man can make it all the way to space, what's stopping you? So, let's break it down and see how you can be the superhero of your town without wearing tights (unless you want to).

Volunteering

First off, have you ever considered volunteering? I've been mentioning it for a reason! It's like joining an exclusive club where you're not only helping others but also leveling up your own skills. Look for something that makes your heart race a bit. Maybe it's helping at a local animal shelter, planting trees in a park, or coaching kids in sports. While these might seem like chores, they're really opportunities to connect with others and add some serious XP to your social skill stats. Plus, making new friends while you're doing good will feel pretty awesome, don't you think?

Setting Your Own Trend

Alright, let's say you're fed up with the status quo and want to start your own small-scale projects. Maybe you notice that there's a lack of clean spaces for soccer games around your block. Why not gather your crew and organize a weekend cleanup? It doesn't just give you a sense of accomplishment; it also sets a cool example for others around you. Remember, every big wave starts as a ripple. When you kick things off, you might inspire others to do the same, and soon, you'll have a tsunami of change washing over your 'hood.

Teamwork Makes the Dream Work

Now, here's where teamwork can really be a game-changer. This is like joining the Avengers, but instead of fighting aliens, you're working to amplify positive outcomes in your neighborhood. By collaborating, you combine your strengths with others' talents. Ever heard the saying "two heads are better than one"? It's true. Teaming up means learning from each other, growing as a group, and making even bigger impacts. Whether it's organizing a community basketball tournament or setting up a local recycling drive, you'll find that sharing ideas and resources makes the process smoother and way more fun.

Reflect on Your Involvement

With each good deed, you're building a legacy that's meaningful to you and positively influential on others. But sometimes, we get involved in community efforts and forget to pause and reflect on our actions. Reflecting lets you look back and see how much you've actually achieved. Take time to think about the long-term impact of what you've done. How do you want people to remember your contribution? Your actions can plant seeds of kindness and service that grow into tall oaks of respect and inspiration for the next gen.

———

⛹ EQ EXERCISE: EMPATHY IN ACTION

Now, if you're thinking, This sounds epic, but how do I even start? Well, here's a rad guideline to help you get rolling:

> Romans 12:15 teaches us to be emotionally attuned to others and to use our strengths to support them. This verse tells us to "rejoice with those who rejoice; mourn with those who mourn" (NIV, 2011/1978). So, I want you to practice using your strengths to empathize with and support a friend or family member who's going through a tough time.

This builds your emotional muscles so that you can handle life's squats and lifts with ease. Get to know what the other person is dealing with, offer to help out, or just be there to listen. You'll be surprised how much of a difference showing kindness and understanding can make.

And hey, why stop here? Think of yourself as a builder, laying down bricks for a future that benefits not just you but everyone around you. The key is starting today, no matter how small your first step is. In time, your actions will inspire others, creating a chain reaction of positivity. You might even end up crafting stories of change and transformation—yours and the community's—that echo for years to come.

MINDSET PRACTICE:
DAILY IMPACT CHALLENGE

Matthew 5:16 says, "In the same way, let your light shine before others, that they may see your good deeds and glorify your Father in heaven" (NIV, 2011/1978). These words encourage us to actively demonstrate our faith through our actions. With that in mind, I want you to complete the following exercise:

Each day for a week, use one of your strengths to positively impact someone in your family, friend group, school, or community. To really drive it home, use your journal to reflect on how it made you feel and how you can keep making a difference.

INTROSPECTIVE JOURNALING
LEGACY BUILDER

"You are the light of the world. A town built on a hill cannot be hidden" (NIV, 2011/1978, Matthew 5:14). This verse reminds us of our potential to make a lasting impact. In this spirit, try the following exercise:

Write about the legacy you want to leave in each area of your life (family, friends, school, community).

INTROSPECTIVE JOURNALING
LEGACY BUILDER

"You are the light of the world. A town built on a hill cannot be hidden" (NIV, 2011/1978, Matthew 5:14). This verse reminds us of our potential to make a lasting impact. In this spirit, try the following exercise:

Reflect on how you can use your strengths to build that legacy starting now.

LET'S BRING IT IN

It's been quite the journey, exploring how tapping into your strengths can sprinkle a bit of magic into everyday life. We've dived headfirst into recognizing how these God-given talents transform mundane activities into meaningful ones and how using them supercharges relationships with empathy and openness. Whether you're solving family dinner dilemmas or transforming social gatherings into grand adventures, each moment is an opportunity to live out your faith and build connections. And let's not forget those challenges—they're like life's gym sessions, building spiritual muscles that empower you to rise above and conquer each level.

Now, as you step into the real world equipped with your unique talents, remember your potential to create positive ripples in your community. Whether you're volunteering or launching neighborhood projects, every action counts. Teaming up with others amplifies these efforts, turning individual strengths into collective victories. By practicing empathy, celebrating achievements, and nurturing community ties, you're setting the stage for lasting change. So, go ahead, show off those strengths, chase those dreams, and watch as your faith-filled actions echo throughout your world, inspiring a wave of positivity and connection.

You're now equipped and ready to flex your growing spiritual muscles! Remember, every small act of kindness and every moment you use your strengths for good is building God's kingdom. Keep shining your light and making a difference.

THE SECOND QUARTER PRAYER

PERSONAL DEVELOPMENT

Heavenly Coach, as I develop my spiritual muscles, remind me that "I can do all this through him who gives me strength" (NIV, 2011/1978, Philippians 4:13). Thank You for the gifts and talents You've given me. Help me train hard in both character and faith. Empower me to push beyond my comfort zone to become the player You designed me to be. I'm excited to discover my position on Your team and grateful for Your patience as I learn and grow. Guide me to use my strengths for Your glory and help me turn my weaknesses into opportunities for growth. Let me play with purpose, knowing You're developing me for something bigger than myself. Amen.

PART THREE
TACKLING LIFE'S CHALLENGES (THE TEENAGE OBSTACLE COURSE)

THE THIRD QUARTER

TACKLING LIFE'S CHALLENGES

(THE TEENAGE OBSTACLE COURSE)

God doesn't call the qualified.
He qualifies the called.
– Mark Batterson

CHAPTER 9
PEER PRESSURE JUJITSU: FLIPPING THE SCRIPT ON NEGATIVE INFLUENCES

Be on your guard; stand firm in the faith;
be courageous; be strong.
–1 Corinthians 16:13

MASTERING peer pressure jujitsu is all about becoming a martial artist of sorts and learning how to skillfully dodge negative influences with the precision of a black belt. This chapter is filled with clever tactics you can use for turning peer-induced stress into personal empowerment, just like in jujitsu, where you use your opponent's strength against them. It's not about fighting back with aggression but rather using wit and humor—imagine Bruce Lee meets stand-up comedy—to gracefully transform negativity into positivity.

Let's say you're just chilling at a party, but the weight of expectations is hovering over you like a fog machine on overdrive. One moment, you're enjoying tortilla chips; the next, you're cast in an unplanned role-play called "Will They Say Yes?" To work this script, you have to learn to dish out bangers faster than a comedian at open mic night, proving that, sometimes, laughter really is the best defense.

Now, let's take a sneak peek at what's in store within this chapter. We're doing a deep dive into a whole bunch of strategies for identifying peer pressure. Much like spotting Waldo in a sea of stripes, you'll learn how to identify those stealthy pressure points that aren't quite as obvious as a drum roll before a magician's trick. On the topic of magic shows, we'll also explore practical techniques that use misdirection as your ally. Instead of disappearing in a puff of smoke when those negative influences pop up, you'll emerge with skills to suggest positive alternatives that are just as lit.

Plus, you'll see how friendships can become your safety net instead of a high-wire act without a harness. With these life hacks, you'll draft your own all-star team who will uplift rather than undermine you. By the end of this chapter, you'll be equipped to say no with finesse, ensuring your values resonate loudly and clearly even with all the loud noise of teen life. Get ready to walk the path from peer follower to peer leader, all while wielding the power of humor and genuine connection.

Life Hacks for Swerving Negative Peer Pressure

There you are, in the middle of a social sparring match. You're surrounded by your classmates, and suddenly, one of them suggests doing something you know doesn't really gel with your values. This is the moment when your peer pressure radar needs to kick in. Clocking those danger points in social interactions is like mapping out the battlefield; it's crucial to know where and when the pressure is coming from so that you can prepare your defenses.

Identifying Pressure Points

Learning to recognize the specific situations or people that create negative peer pressure is very important. It's rarely as obvious as a flashing neon sign saying, "Pressure Ahead!" Often, it's subtle, like a sly comment suggesting everyone's doing it (whatever "it" may be) or getting the side-eye of judgment if you don't join in. One way to sharpen your senses is to pay attention to your gut feeling. If something feels off, it's probably time to reassess the situation.

Not all pressure is bad, though. Sometimes, your friends might encourage you to study harder or try out for a team, which could be positive peer pressure pushing you toward growth. But when it veers into negative territory, that's your cue to tap into some mental jujitsu techniques.

Flip the Script

Speaking of jujitsu, let's take a page from martial arts. The beauty of jujitsu lies in its ability to use an opponent's strength against them. Similarly, when someone tries to pressure you into doing something that doesn't feel right, flip the script on them. For example, if you're invited to ditch class with your squad, maybe you can suggest a fun group study session followed by a movie night. This move not only redirects the negativity but also frames you as a leader who makes cool and smart choices.

Crack a Joke

And don't sleep on humor as a technique. Say you're at a party, and someone offers you a drink, but you're just not into it. With a playful smile, say, "Nah, I'm good. I've got plans to win an award for being the most hydrated person in the room!" Humor can mellow out tension, making it easier to stand your ground without making others feel like you've got them on the ropes.

Curate Your Crew

A healthy squad of homies can also act as your safety net in situations where negative peer pressure has you feeling some type of way. Positive ride-or-dies can make sticking to respectful behavior easier, showing that kindness isn't uncool but actually super powerful. Just like superheroes have their league, having a crew that shares your values and interests means you've got backup whenever you need it. These are the friends who'll cheer you on, respect your decisions, and always have your back.

Creating this support network isn't about assembling a massive entourage—quality over quantity wins every time. Look for connections based on shared values and mutual respect. It could be the people you meet at a club focused on hobbies you love, a sports team, or a volunteer group passionate about making a difference. The secret sauce is mutual encouragement and building each other up rather than tearing anyone down.

Saying No Like a Pro

Now, onto the grand finale: developing the self-awareness and confidence to say no like you're throwing down a wrestling mat of pure certainty. Being aware of your limits and recognizing when something doesn't vibe with your personal values takes practice, but it's a skill worth leveling up. It starts with understanding who you are—your values, what matters to you, and what doesn't. Once you've got that down, declining becomes less of a buzzkill and more of an epic declaration.

You might be wondering, *What if saying no makes things awkward?* Sure, it might go down like that. But true power lies in the delivery. Practicing assertive communication can turn a lukewarm refusal into a confident one. Use "I" statements to express your feelings without sounding like you're pointing fingers. Before straight up turning someone down, try: "I appreciate the invite, but it's not for me." It's clear, respectful, and gets your point across without inviting further pressure.

And hey, practice makes perfect. Try role-playing scenarios with your homies or fam to build your confidence. Think of it as pep talks for your brain. Over time, you'll find it easier to stand on business and handle social circles without losing yourself in them.

Realigning Approval and Building Positive Friendships

In the wild world of teenage life, where social media and friend circles often set the stage, there's a not-so-secret club that everyone seems to join without realizing it—Peer Pressure Anonymous. It's like a silent agreement that never gets discussed aloud but guides so many actions. It's basically like Fight Club. But what if you could change the game and use these pressures as a stepping stone rather than a stumbling block?

The Art of Approval

First off, let's talk about the art of approval. Many teens feel the need to look for acceptance from friends, which can sometimes turn into a dependency on external validation. But what if instead of looking to others, you looked up—literally? Redirecting this desire for approval toward God can really hook you up with inner peace and self-worth (Datu et al., 2024). It's basically a backstage pass to confidence, where your values and beliefs are headlining acts supported by divine assurance. When you match up your actions with faith-based principles, you're tapping into a source of strength that's unwavering and eternal. This path doesn't just lead to self-acceptance but anchors you in a place where true worth is measured.

———

JOURNALING EXERCISE
THE PRESSURE POINT IDENTIFICATION

In the Bible, 1 Corinthians 15:33 states, "Do not be misled: 'Bad company corrupts good character'" (NIV, 2011/1978). This emphasizes the impact that our social circles have on our character, especially when the company we keep can majorly influence our behavior and decisions in a bad way.

This next exercise aims to help you develop an awareness of your personal vulnerabilities to peer pressure and the mental jujitsu moves you can practice to swerve these pressures. Follow these steps:

01
For one week, maintain a daily log of pressure points, noting situations where you felt pressured to do something against your values.

02
Describe the pressure points —who was involved, what was said, how you felt.

03
Reflect on how you responded and whether your response aligned with your Christian values.

04
Brainstorm alternative responses for similar situations you may encounter in the future, imagining them as jujitsu moves to "flip" the pressure.

JOURNALING EXERCISE
THE PRESSURE POINT IDENTIFICATION

01

For one week, maintain a daily log of pressure points, noting situations where you felt pressured to do something against your values.

JOURNALING EXERCISE
THE PRESSURE POINT IDENTIFICATION

02

Describe the pressure points—who was involved, what was said, how you felt.

JOURNALING EXERCISE
THE PRESSURE POINT IDENTIFICATION

03

Reflect on how you responded and whether your response aligned with your Christian values.

JOURNALING EXERCISE
THE PRESSURE POINT IDENTIFICATION

04

Brainstorm alternative responses for similar situations you may encounter in the future, imagining them as jujitsu moves to "flip" the pressure.

☧ EQ EXERCISE:
THE APPROVAL REDIRECT

Galatians 1:10 says, "Am I now trying to win the approval of human beings, or of God? Or am I trying to please people? If I were still trying to please people, I would not be a servant of Christ" (NIV, 2011/1978). This directly addresses the issue of looking for approval from your squad versus staying true to your faith.

As you go into this exercise, set a mindset goal for yourself to strengthen internal validation and reduce susceptibility to peer pressure by focusing on God's approval. Then, follow these steps:

01

List 5–10 situations where you might be tempted to seek peer approval.

02

For each situation, write down the following:
- what peers might want you to do
- what you believe God would want you to do
- a positive self-affirmation that reinforces your worth in God's eyes

03

Practice saying these affirmations out loud daily.

EQ EXERCISE:
THE APPROVAL REDIRECT

In difficult situations, hit up this chart (even if just in your mind) and use it to redirect your need for approval from others to God. Think of it as your mental workout plan to reframe situations where the pressure to conform feels overwhelming. Each time you're asked to make a choice that tests your values, this chart will help reroute your brain's GPS back to faith-based co-ordinates.

FRIEND INTERACTION
THE UPLIFT CHALLENGE

If you flip to Hebrews 10:24–25 (NIV, 2011/1978), you'll find the following passage:

And let us consider how we may spur one another on toward love and good deeds, not giving up meeting together, as some are in the habit of doing, but encouraging one another—and all the more as you see the Day approaching.

This emphasizes the importance of positive peer influence and mutual encouragement in faith. It's basically all about squad goals. Forget those losers who keep pushing you to wild out; instead, form a crew that's committed to uplifting one another based on positive influence and Christian principles.

For this next exercise, link up with some of your homies or youth group buddies who are committed to positive influence and meet weekly for an upliftment challenge:

01

To start the session, each person will share a challenge they're facing (e.g., academic pressure, temptation, family issues).

02

The group can then brainstorm positive, faith-based ways to handle each challenge.

03

Finish up by setting weekly goals for supporting each other and practicing these positive solutions.

FRIEND INTERACTION
THE UPLIFT CHALLENGE

Next

Use a group chat or social media to share daily encouragement and Scripture. In the next meeting, discuss how you flipped the script on negative influences using your group's support.

> Yo guys!! Big game tomorrow and I'm lowkey hyped 🙌 Just remember - we got this

> Bros. Just read this and had to drop it here - Philippians 4:13 says 'I can do all this through him who gives me strength' 🙏 Like fr... we're not doing this alone. God's got our backs on that field tomorrow 💯

> Not gonna lie I was stressing about tomorrow but you guys just flipped my whole mindset

These exercises will help you develop a mindset that's bulletproof to negative peer pressure and proactive in building positive relationships. Having regular upliftment sessions with your boys can create a sense of community that hypes personal growth alongside spiritual improvement and gives everyone an opportunity to share their wins, struggles, and faith journeys.

Together, you can be that collective force that transforms challenges into vehicles for empowerment. But why stop there? By going deeper with group discussions and setting weekly goals to tackle the hurdles of teen hood as a formidable team, you transform those chats into a wellspring of strength and positivity. Let's say school stress is running high, or drama's unfolding faster than a soap opera. These discussion groups can be safe havens where solutions are thought up, support is shared, and friendships blossom through understanding and respect.

LET'S BRING IT IN

As this chapter draws to a close, imagine yourself in the ring—not with boxing gloves on but kitted out with humor and a solid sense of self. We've journeyed through the wild terrain of peer pressure, and you've learned how to spot it from miles away, much like a fashionista spots a new trend. But instead of falling into the trap of doing things just because everyone else is, you now have the tools to flip that scenario into an opportunity for positive power moves. Whether it's planning a group study session over skipping class or tossing out a witty line about prize-winning hydration levels, you've got the secret sauce to turning potential pitfalls into chances to shine.

Think of your newfound skills as just one more superpower, but this one gives you the ability to transform peer pressure into a source of personal growth. It can help you build a squad that has your back and align with values that really resonate with you. It's not about joining the biggest team; it's about finding your league of extraordinary buddies who own at respect and kindness while having a blast. As you move forward, remember: It's cool to be kind, fun to be formidable, and pretty lit to stand by what you believe in.

I'll leave you with this thought: True strength isn't about never feeling pressure; it's about knowing how to swat it away when it comes. You've got the moves now, champ. Keep practicing these techniques and watch how God transforms you into a positive influence on those around you.

CHAPTER 10
SOCIAL MEDIA SURVIVAL GUIDE: NAVIGATING THE DIGITAL JUNGLE

Be on your guard; stand firm in the faith; be courageous; be strong. –1
Corinthians 16:13

NAVIGATING social media is a battle many of us fight on the daily. Much like wading through an actual jungle, where every swinging vine and hidden creature could either be an ally or adversary, the digital landscape is filled with experiences that can either hype or hurt you. The likes, shares, and comments are a magnet, pulling you into a world that's both thrilling and treacherous. You click on one video, then another, and before you know it, you've gone down the rabbit hole. You lose hours in this engaging abyss, and when you emerge, you're left questioning how something so virtual can feel so real.

In this chapter, I'll be kitting you out with cheat codes that you can use to safely explore and thrive in this online environment without losing yourself in the process. You'll uncover ways to maintain clear-headedness and maybe even reconnect with a sense of faith while scrolling through endless feeds. From understanding the psychological effects of your screen addiction to managing the anxiety of FOMO, you'll learn to make conscious choices about what you engage with. Aside from helping you reclaim the joy and meaning that real-life connections offer, I'll also help you make sure your time spent online genuinely improves your life rather than takes away from it.

Getting the Lowdown on Social Media's Psychological Effects

So, you've just created a fire new post on your favorite social media platform, and every little red heart or thumbs-up you receive gives you a buzz of happiness. Feels great, doesn't it? That's exactly what social media platforms are counting on. They are like slot machines, specifically designed to trigger your brain's reward system.

Whenever you get a like or a share, your brain releases dopamine, the "feel good" chemical (Sperling, 2024). It's that same rush you might get from chowing down on a delicious slice of pizza or finally beating your high score in a video game. But here's the catch: This cycle of instant gratification can make social media addictive, keeping you glued to your screen for longer than you planned.

The Fear of Missing Out

Now, let's talk about FOMO, otherwise known as fear of missing out. Ever find yourself checking your phone every five seconds because you're worried something's popping off without you? You're not alone. Many teens experience this electronic itch that needs constant scratching (Saba, 2024). The irony is that while you're busy living through a screen, real life is slipping through your fingers. While you could be enjoying your time at the park or focusing on your hobbies, you're worried about updates and notifi-cations. That nagging feeling that you're missing out does more than distract; it sows seeds of anxiety that can grow into bigger mental health issues if left unchecked.

Filtering Out Reality

And if FOMO's not enough, there's the land of Insta vs. reality. We've all seen them, those impossibly perfect pictures floating around on social media. From flawless selfies to snapshots of dream vacations, everything looks picture-perfect. But let's be real: Most of these images are heavily tweaked with filters and edits. These curated posts create unrealistic standards that no one can actually live up to, totally warping our perceptions of what life should look like. Seeing these "perfect" lives makes average days seem so lame by comparison, leading to self-esteem issues and feelings of not being good enough.

A Digital Detox Is a Game-Changer

So, how do you swerve this digital jungle's negative effects? Enter a digital detox. Trust me, it's not as scary as it sounds! It just means taking a break from screen time and replacing it with activi-ties that benefit you in other ways. It doesn't mean quitting cold turkey; you're just hitting pause to give yourself some breathing room. Disconnect from the internet and reconnect with the real world. Spend time catching up with your homies face-to-face, go touch some grass, pick up a book, or dive into a hobby.

By stepping away from the screen, even for just a bit, you'll find it's easier to connect with the world around you and spark genuine connections. You'll get to link up with friends for an afternoon hike or play a game of touch football without being distracted by your phone buzzing nonstop in your pocket. These moments enhance your personal growth and deepen bonds with others far beyond what any app can offer.

And there's another bonus: After a digital detox, when you make a comeback on social media, you do so with a clearer mind, using it intentionally rather than just out of habit.

Here's an easy guideline to get started on your FOMO detox journey:

- Aim for small, manageable breaks to begin with, like setting aside an hour each day for no screens.
- Use this time to do things that bring you joy without digital interference.
- Gradually increase your detox periods over time.

The goal is to shift your focus back to real-world experiences, improving them while still maintaining a healthy relationship with your devices.

Navigating Social Media While Upholding Christian Values

You're diving into the vast ocean of social media, where memes ride on waves, viral videos pop up like sea creatures, and hashtags gather in schools. It's easy to get swept away if you're not anchoring yourself with strong, positive values. As a Christian teen, it's so important for you to engage with content that mirrors the virtues highlighted in Philippians 4:8—things that are true, noble, right, pure, lovely, admirable, and excellent or praiseworthy. How can you make sure that your time spent online uplifts rather than drags you down? I'm so glad you asked!

Become a Content Curator

First, consider every interaction you encounter online. Much like choosing the perfect songs to go on a playlist for a road trip, curate your social media feed with awareness. It's like composing a symphony of positivity and authenticity. If a piece of content feels out of tune with your values, it might be time to mute, unfollow, or just keep scrolling.

While it might be tempting to click on whatever catches your eye, remember that your digital diet directly impacts your thoughts and attitudes. As you sift through posts, focus on those that resonate with faith-filled values instead of the noise of negativity.

Make It Meaningful

Meaningful online interactions can also make your digital experience so much better. Social media doesn't have to just be about counting likes or followers; it's an opportunity to build relationships that encourage and nurture faith. These connections should serve as constant reminders of God's grace, giving you a network of support when you're feeling shaky in your beliefs. Share your wins, challenges, and struggles with friends who have the same values, and watch as these bonds strengthen your resolve to live authentically.

———

INTERACTIVE SECTION:
GAME PLAN HUDDLE

Do not be misled: 'Bad company corrupts good character'" (NIV, 2011/1978, 1 Corinthians 15:33). You might recall this verse from Chapter 9, where we discussed peer pressure. It's also especially relevant to the temptations and falsehoods on social media, where you are constantly exposed to various influences.

This piece of Scripture warns against the negative impact of associating with the wrong crowd, whether online or offline. It serves as a reminder to be cautious about the content you consume and the people you interact with on social platforms.

Taking this as inspiration, try the following exercise with a parent or mentor to make sure your skills are up to scratch:

01

Share a recent challenge you faced and how you handled it.

02

Discuss strategies for staying true to your faith in difficult situations.

03

Role-play scenarios dealing with peer pressure or social media conflicts.

JOURNALING EXERCISE:
THE DIGITAL COMPASS CHECK

Earlier, I mentioned Philippians 4:8, which states, **"Finally, brothers and sisters, whatever is true, whatever is noble, whatever is right, whatever is pure, whatever is lovely, whatever is admirable—if anything is excellent or praiseworthy—think about such things"** (NIV, 2011/1978). This passage gives us a framework for evaluating the content we consume, which is highly relevant to social media use.

For this next exercise, complete the following steps in your journal:

01

Log your daily social media or mobile use, taking note of the time spent online and your main activities.

02

For each platform or significant interaction, rate it based on the criteria in Philippians 4:8. Was there truth, nobility, rightness, purity, loveliness, or admirability?

03

Reflect on how your social media use aligns with these values on a broader level.

04

Set weekly goals to adjust your "digital compass" toward more positive content and interactions.

JOURNALING EXERCISE:
THE DIGITAL COMPASS CHECK

My Daily Digital Log

Time	Activity	Rating

My Weekly Goals for more positive content and interactions

EQ PRACTICE:
THE DOPAMINE DETOX CHALLENGE

"For where your treasure is, there your heart will be also," (NIV, 2011/1978, Matthew 6:21). This verse speaks to what you value most, which is relevant to the addictive nature of social media likes and followers. It encourages you to examine where you're investing your time and emotions—the focus of our final exercise for the chapter.

To complete this exercise, complete these steps:

01

Choose one day a week for a "social media fast." During this time, do things that align with your values and faith.

02

Each hour, rate your mood and any urges you might feel to check social media.

03

At the end of the day, reflect on what you learned about your dependence on digital validation.

04

Gradually increase the duration of these "fasts" over time.

EQ PRACTICE:
THE DOPAMINE DETOX CHALLENGE

"For where your treasure is, there your heart will be also," (NIV, 2011/1978, Matthew 6:21). This verse speaks to what you value most, which is relevant to the addictive nature of social media likes and followers. It encourages you to examine where you're investing your time and emotions—the focus of our final exercise for the chapter.

LET'S BRING IT IN

Navigating social media can feel like trying to find your way through a maze with a blindfold on, especially when you're trying to keep your faith front and center. We've wandered through a digital forest of dopamine hits, FOMO, and picture-perfect illusions. But understanding these online traps is only half the battle. Now, it's time to whip out the trusty map you've just obtained—a plan filled with epic life hacks that you can use to avoid getting lost in the noise. Whether it's taking a breather through a digital detox or shaping your feed to reflect positive values, these strategies are tools for maintaining clarity and faithfulness in your online adventures. Remember, no app can replace the genuine connections you build IRL, and a well-timed break might just be what you need to reset both mind and spirit.

But the adventure doesn't stop at unplugging every now and then. As young Christians, throwing a little humor and positivity into your online interactions can be a game-changer. Imagine treating each post, like, or share as an opportunity to shine your light. When faced with the temptation to jump onto the bandwagon, embrace the challenge of choosing content that aligns with your beliefs, even if it means going against the tide. Laughter and faith go hand in hand; they make life more colorful and conversations more open. So, channel that energy into making your social media experience a reflection of who you truly are, embracing moments of silliness while holding firm to your values. After all, this isn't just about surviving in a digital world—it's about thriving with purpose and joy. And always remember, you're called to be a light in the digital darkness, not just another face in the filtered crowd.

CHAPTER 11
DATING 101: GOD'S HEART SMART GUIDE

Above all else, guard your heart,
for everything you do flows from it.
–Proverbs 4:23

DATING CAN BE PRETTY HECTIC, especially when you're looking for something more than just swiping left and right. But what does it mean to date like a pro, God's way? No, it doesn't involve saying "hallelujah" after every sentence or turning your dates into Sunday school lessons! It's about finding your way on this exciting path while staying true to your values and beliefs. It's about looking for meaningful connections that respect both your heart and your faith and doing it with a smile (and maybe the occasional awkward laugh because, let's be real, dating can get a little weird sometimes).

This chapter is here to give you not just advice but encouragement, laughter, and reflection. As we get started, prepare yourself for valuable insights into building relationships that honor God and a bit of soul-searching along the way. From understanding how to guard your heart without locking it in a tower to setting boundaries that are more than just imaginary lines in the sand, this chapter covers it all. We'll also explore the importance of practicing humility even when you're tempted by the last slice of pizza, how journaling can help you stay emotionally aware, and why group dating isn't just for shy guys or those stuck in 2005.

You'll also find practical tips on how to get through those tough conversations about relationship expectations and how keeping them light-hearted with a sprinkle of humor can go a long way. Plus, there's a whole bunch of stuff about building respect and genuine connection, making the process of dating less of a cringe-fest and more of an adventure grounded in faith. By taking these steps, you're not just learning about love; you're creating a story of growth and discovery—one blessed date at a time.

Dating With Christian Values

Dating can be filled with excitement, but when your compass is set toward God-honoring relationships, the path you take becomes even more meaningful. Throwing your Christian values into dating involves understanding the emotions that guide you, setting boundaries, and prioritizing respect and humility.

Guard Your Heart

First up, let's talk about the heart. You know, that thing that beats faster every time your crush walks by. Guarding your heart isn't about turning into a love Scrooge; it's more about being mindful of your emotions because they majorly influence your actions and decisions in relationships.

Proverbs 4:23 drops some serious bars when it says, "Above all else, guard your heart, for everything you do flows from it" (*NIV*, 2011/1978). This verse suggests that protecting your emotions is a pretty important part of maintaining healthy connections. It's like having a shield—not one that blocks all feelings out but one that guarantees that only the good stuff, grounded in God's love, gets through.

So, how do you clock these emotional influences? With some old-school journaling! It's like detective work but with fewer trench coats and more reflecting on what connects with Christian teachings. Each entry helps you uncover patterns in how you react emotionally within relationships. Let's say jealousy creeps up. Jot it down and reflect on how to turn that green-eyed monster back into a calm, trusting soul. By journaling on the regular, you'll start seeing how your emotions sync—or sometimes clash—with your faith.

Biblical Boundaries

Now, speaking of staying in line, let's have a chat about boundaries, the secret ingredient in respectful and committed relationships. Biblical principles give us a solid foundation on how to establish them. The idea isn't to build walls but to define what is important to you in a relationship. Boundaries protect your heart and mind, ensuring that you're not letting just anyone waltz in and rummage around. You're basically creating a guideline of dos and don'ts customized just for you and your bae—no gate-crashers allowed!

Setting boundaries right from the start prevents Heartbreak City from becoming a regular stop on your dating route. Here's a simple way to get started: Think of the talk where you define the relationship as a necessary checkpoint. It's not as deep as it sounds—it's just a conversation about what you both expect and need. This is the moment to decide things like whether you're comfortable hanging out alone at each other's houses or if sharing every date-night detail on social media is a deal-breaker.

Respect and Humility

Besides guarding your heart and setting those super important boundaries, showing respect and humility goes a long way. Respect isn't just about holding doors open—though props if you do. It's also about valuing the other person's thoughts, feelings, and space. If you want to improve, a practical exercise might involve acting out scenarios where you practice responding with grace in situations that require patience and understanding.

Let's say you're out on a date, and your special someone goes in for the last slice of your favorite pizza. Instead of duking it out for the final piece, practicing humility would mean smiling, letting it slide, and maybe even ordering another round. Relationships are built on mutual support and appreciation. It's the little things that nurture a deeper connection that's rooted in Godly love.

While we're chatting about keeping things fun and light-hearted, the key here is making sure your dates are enjoyable without losing track of your commitment to God. So, yes, date with a mission. Enjoy the journey and have fun but always keep the bigger picture in mind: finding someone who respects your beliefs and dreams and is ready to share in that joy.

Group Dates, Because Third Wheeling Is Actually Cool (and Smart)

There you are, surrounded by your friends—and a special someone—at a legendary game night, laughter echoing off the walls as you battle it out for victory through another round of charades. While this sounds like a fun evening (and it is), it's also a life hack for dating that aligns with Christian values.

In today's whirlwind dating scene, people are really sleeping on group dating, but when done right, it can create an environment where companionship flourishes and mutual support becomes second nature. Involving friends changes the game when it comes to what it means to seek love. It supports the idea that dating doesn't have to be a solo venture filled with anxiety and guess-work. It can be a collective journey toward understanding both yourself and others through the lens of faith.

Group dating is a unique opportunity for building healthy relationships grounded in faith. By bringing your homies along, you create a network of support that sticks to your beliefs. This vibe allows you and the person you're interested in to scope each other out in different social contexts, leading to more genuine connec-tions without the usual pressures you find in traditional dating.

Aside from being fun, participating in group activities is also a demonstration of living your faith. It encourages openness, honest communication, and shared learning moments that lead to enduring connections. In this space, there's room to discuss important topics, share personal stories, and provide encouragement rooted in respect.

Supporting one another in a group setting also emphasizes the importance of accountability. Having others witness your interactions with the person you're connecting with is a gentle reminder to maintain behaviors that uphold Christian ethics. This dynamic creates a balanced environment where everyone feels valued and heard, reinforcing those critical lessons taught in youth groups or Sunday school.

So, with all that said, you're probably wondering what a group date looks like. Think beyond the typical "dinner and a movie" scenario. Do things that promote teamwork and solidarity. Maybe you can try something like organizing a hike, a community service outing, or even a potluck dinner where everyone brings a dish. Similarly, doing things that reinforce faith-based principles, like attending church events or Bible study groups together, invites God into your relationships. This is where respect, love, and understanding take center stage, allowing these virtues to permeate throughout your interactions.

———

JOURNALING EXERCISE
THE HEART CHECK

I mentioned Proverbs 4:23 earlier and how it emphasizes the importance of protecting your heart, which, in biblical terms, refers to the center of emotions, thoughts, and decisions. When it comes to dating, this verse is a reminder to be careful about who you allow to influence your feelings and choices. To put this into practice, try the following exercise:

For a week, spend 10 minutes each day reflecting on your emotions and thoughts about relationships.

Write down any patterns you notice in your attractions or crushes.

JOURNALING EXERCISE
THE HEART CHECK

Ask yourself: Are these feelings aligned with the values described in Philippians 4:8 (truth, nobility, rightness, purity, loveliness, admirability)?

At the end of the week, review your entries and find areas where you might need to guard your heart more carefully.

EQ PRACTICE:
THE RESPECT SIMULATOR

Philippians 2:3 states, **"Do nothing out of selfish ambition or vain conceit. Rather, in humility, value others above yourselves"** (NIV, 2011/1978). This teaches us the importance of staying humble and valuing others, which is pretty important in romantic relationships. It encourages a mindset of mutual respect and consideration.

With this verse in mind, try this exercise:

Create a list of 3-5 hypothetical dating scenarios that might challenge your ability to show respect (e.g., disagreements, differing opinions, or temptations).

For each scenario, write down three possible responses: 1) one selfish, 2) one neutral, and 3) one that demonstrates respect for the other person

1.

2.

3.

4.

5.

EQ PRACTICE:
THE RESPECT SIMULATOR

01

Practice visualizing yourself choosing the respectful response in real-life situations.

02

Reflect on how each response aligns with the biblical principle of valuing others above yourself...

Situations

My reflections

1.

2.

3.

FRIEND INTERACTION:
THE GROUP DATE BRAINSTORM BASH

"And let us consider how we may spur one another on toward love and good deeds, not giving up meeting together, as some are in the habit of doing but encouraging one another" (NIV, 2011/1978, Hebrews 10:24-25). As you can see from this quote, the Bible encourages believers to meet together and support each other, which aligns well with the concept of group dating and fostering positive social interactions.

To make group dating a fun, collaborative experience that strengthens friendships and creates opportunities for genuine connection, try this exercise with your squad:

01

Get together (in person or virtually) with snacks and good vibes. Then, ask each person to suggest one group date idea that
- is budget-friendly
- allows for conversation
- aligns with your shared values

02

Vote on the top three ideas, then plan these group dates after assigning roles (e.g., organizer, snack master, hype person).

03

After each date, have a quick debrief:
- What worked well?
- What could be improved?
- How did it help you get to know each other better?

JOURNALING EXERCISE:
THE SQUAD-DATE DIARY

Ecclesiastes 4:9-10 (NIV, 2011/1978) emphasizes the value of companionship and mutual support: "Two are better than one, because they have a good return for their labor: If either of them falls down, one can help the other up." You can see how relevant this is when it comes to the concept of group dating.

This next exercise lets you reflect on your interactions, document experiences, and learn from them. Writing down your perceptions about how you and others express empathy, humor, and kindness is a great opportunity to grow emotionally and spiritually. It turns every date into a learning experience, helping you understand your reactions and feelings within a group setting.

To complete this activity, plan and participate in at least one group date per week. After each outing, jot down

the squad's vibe

one thing you learned about each person

a moment when the group dynamic made things less awkward

how the experience synced with your Christian values

At the end of the month, reflect on how group dating has impacted your social life and understanding of relationships.

LET'S BRING IT IN

Using your Christian values to guide you through your relationships might seem like a lot to ask, but as you've seen, it's more about setting the right course than memorizing a rulebook. We've talked about guarding your heart without turning into an ice king and setting boundaries that are less about building walls and more about defining what feels right for you. Now, you know that those heart-protecting shields are not there to keep love out; they're there to make sure that only the good stuff gets through—a bit like checking your tickets before boarding the love train. And let's not forget the importance of respect and humility, which turn sharing the last slice of pizza into a moment of connection instead of a fight to the death.

Then there's the whole group dating thing—a squad adventure is way more exciting than riding solo! We've dived into how this setup can totally turn dating into a team sport rather than a high-stakes chess game. By rolling with your crew, you keep things light, learn a ton, and discover how your faith shines in different settings. It's an opportunity to create good vibes and establish a setting where laughter echoes and Christian values become second nature. Having each other's backs strengthens accountability and sprinkles every date with purpose.

As you take these steps, keep in mind that dating is not just a quest for a perfect partner but a journey of understanding yourself and others through a lens of faith. Dating doesn't have to be a game of hit or miss. With God's wisdom as your guide and these principles as your guardrails, you're set to build relationships that honor both God and the people you care about.

CHAPTER 12

FEARLESS: STEPPING OUT OF YOUR COMFORT ZONE

For the Spirit God gave us does not make us timid,
but gives us power, love and self-discipline.
–2 Timothy 1:7

STEPPING out of your comfort zone is like swapping your trusty old blanket for a superhero cape. Sure, the idea might seem a bit scary at first—goodbye cozy couch, hello world-saving adventures —but that's the most exciting part! In this chapter, we'll dive head-first into what it means to be fearless, pushing past those snug boundaries and embracing the unknown with the kind of hyped-up enthusiasm usually reserved for Saturday morning cartoons. From battling self-doubt dragons to tapping into powers you didn't even know you had, we're gearing up for an adventure that promises growth, fun, and maybe even a little bit of heroics.

Along the way, you'll discover how crushing self-doubt is a transformative step in becoming a more confident, courageous you. We'll explore everything from trusting in divine guidance (because, let's face it, having faith in something bigger than yourself can be transformative) to practical steps like keeping a courage journal. The aim here isn't just to challenge you but to kit you out with the mindset and tools needed to take on life's quests with enthusiasm and finesse. Think of this chapter as your guidebook to becoming, well, the most lit version of your super-self. Ready to leap into action? Your adventure starts now!

Crushing Self-Doubt and Embracing Courage

You're standing at the edge of a swimming pool, muscles tensed and toes gripping the edge like it's the last bar of chocolate on Earth. That's where self-doubt lives: in that moment right before you leap. It's when your mind starts whispering all sorts of wild things like, *Are you sure you can swim? What if there's a sea monster with a weird rubber duck obsession down there?*

Self-doubt is a sneaky little bugger that likes to hang around and keep you from experiencing the thrill and growth that lies just beyond the jump. But don't sweat it, fam. Developing the courage to overcome this pesky hurdle is not only doable but also your golden ticket to a more awesome version of yourself.

Don't Let Self-Doubt Do You Dirty

First off, let's get one thing straight: Self-doubt isn't some alien invasion, but it does hit you with some annoying roadblocks in your journey. It gets in the way of your personal growth by keeping you sheltered in your comfort zone, like a koala clinging to its eucalyptus tree. Embracing new experiences takes a bit of courage. Trust me, I know. But try to imagine each new experience as a major mission in your favorite video game. With each one you conquer, you're leveling up your confidence and gaining mad skills that contribute to your character's development—except here, the character is you. Seemingly small moments, like joining a new club, trying out for the school play, or speaking in front of a crowd, add up to form an epic highlight reel of your life.

God's Got Your Back

Now, here's a life hack for facing those fearsome foes: divine guidance. Channeling your inner faith means trusting that God's got your back, even when you feel like you're wrestling three-headed dragons of doubt. The Bible also backs you up with some nuggets of wisdom about crushing fear, like Philippians 4:13, which says, "I can do all this through him who gives me strength" (*NIV*, 2011/1978). Leaning into this belief isn't about dodging the tough stuff; it's about being empowered to face the world as the unique and incredible legend God created you to be. So, grab your metaphorical sword of faith and forge ahead with courage!

Give Yourself a Shoutout

Let's not forget about celebrating your wins along the way. Every milestone you reach deserves a shoutout; it doesn't matter whether it's leaping into the unknown or just dipping a toe in. Treat yourself to something nice, like a smoothie or 10 minutes of cat videos—whatever your vibe is. Celebrating achievements, even small ones, builds momentum and gets you hyped for knocking down future walls of doubt. It's like fueling your inner adventurer with high fives and confetti.

Courage in All shapes and Sizes

Now, while you're diving headfirst into unfamiliar waters,

remember that courage can come in different sizes. Not everyone is born with a lion's roar, but that doesn't matter. What matters is that you take a step, any step, even if it feels small. Maybe today it's raising your hand in class; tomorrow, it could be starting that YouTube channel you've been dreaming of since forever ago. Each act, no matter the size, contributes to your growth and hooks you up with the courage needed to handle bigger leaps.

Let Your People Know

Last but definitely not least, communicate openly with your parents and any relevant authority figures about your goals and fears. They're like the pit crew in your Formula 1 race: ready with advice, support, and maybe snacks (chocolate chip cookies, anyone?). They're the team of cheerleaders that will inspire you to climb higher and dare more boldly. Sharing your journey with them not only keeps them in the loop but also helps you get some valuable feedback and encouragement.

Cultivating a Growth Mindset Through Exploration

Stepping out of your comfort zone is similar to trading in a well-worn pair of slippers for some sturdy hiking boots. Yes, it might be uncomfortable at first, but every step taken in those fresh kicks brings you closer to discovering new peaks and valleys of potential. Let's figure out how you can adopt a growth mindset that sees challenges not as roadblocks or mud puddles but as opportunities for learning.

Seeing the Opportunities in Challenges

Seeing challenges as opportunities can be the secret ingredient to leveling up your resilience and adaptability. Again, think about it like playing a video game: Every level throws tougher enemies and more complex puzzles your way. But what happens when you beat a level? You gain experience, new skills, and a badge of honor that shows you've aced that challenge. Life is pretty much the same. When you face a challenge head-on and see it as a chance to learn, you develop the ability to bounce back stronger than before. It's like gaining an extra life or a power-up; you come away with more tools to tackle future obstacles, ready to adapt to whatever life throws your way.

Give Yourself Grace

Practically speaking, though, how do you expand your comfort zone? Start small and acknowledge each step forward. Remember, Rome wasn't built in a day, so neither will your fortress of confidence be. Maybe this week, you can set yourself the goal of sitting at a different lunch table, striking up a conversation with someone new, or volunteering to lead a group project. Every deliberate action you take, no matter how minor, contributes to your growth. And here's a sweet hack: Track these wins in your journal. This gives you tangible evidence of progress and also serves as a reminder of how far you've come when you hit a snag.

One Step at a Time

Try to get into the habit of regularly pushing your boundaries through specific actions. This leads to sustained growth and empowerment. Each step is a seed you plant; with time and nurture, it will grow into a mighty tree. Sure, it takes effort and patience, but the shade it provides and the fruits it bears make the journey worthwhile. Over time, these experiences all add up and form a strong foundation, empowering you to take on bigger challenges with confidence and grace.

To wrap it all up without tying a too-perfect bow (because, really, when does life ever finish that neatly?), remember that stepping beyond your comfort zone doesn't mean leaping blindly into the unknown. It means approaching challenges with open arms and a heart full of faith. It means recognizing that discomfort and failure aren't the opposite of success—they're important parts of the process. Embrace the awkward stumbles and missteps as part of your learning curve. They're proof that you're moving forward, doing the work, and, most importantly, growing.

———

JOURNALING EXERCISE:
THE COURAGE CHRONICLES

In Joshua 1:9, the Lord reminds us that He is always with us, giving us the strength and courage we need to face new challenges. He says, "**Have I not commanded you? Be strong and courageous. Do not be afraid; do not be discouraged, for the Lord your God will be with you wherever you go**" (NIV, 2011/1978). This message is relevant when it comes to stepping outside your comfort zone because it assures you of divine support in everything you do.

Okay, but let's say facing your fears feels harder than patting your head and rubbing your stomach at the same time. How do you summon the courage? Enter a journaling experiment destined to become your BFF on this journey:

1. Each day, write down one thing that scares you or that would push you out of your comfort zone.

2. Next to each fear, write a short prayer asking for God's guidance and strength.

<u>Day 1</u>

<u>Day 2</u>

<u>Day 3</u>

<u>Day 4</u>

JOURNALING EXERCISE:
THE COURAGE CHRONICLES

Challenge yourself to face one of these fears every week.

4. After facing the fear, journal about...

- how you felt before, during, and after
- where you felt God's presence in the experience
- what you learned about yourself

At the end of each month, reflect on your growth and the fears you've conquered.

Think of this as your personal logbook of bravery. Tried sushi for the first time? Write it down. Spoke up in class? Count that, too. These entries are glimpses into how far you've ventured. In moments of weakness, they remind you of how far you've come.

EQ PRACTICE:
THE COMFORT ZONE CARTOGRAPHER

Proverbs 3:5-6 (NIV, 2011/1978) says, **"Trust in the Lord with all your heart and lean not on your own understanding; in all your ways submit to him, and he will make your paths straight**." This message encourages you to trust in God's guidance rather than relying only on your own understanding; it also serves as a reminder to look for God's direction when you face new and challenging experiences.

For this EQ practice, picture yourself as an explorer charting unknown territory on a map. Your comfort zone is the safe, cozy area you've already ventured into. Beyond that are the lands of opportunity and personal growth waiting to be discovered. Visualizing these areas allows you to figure out the specific spots where you want to expand and develop and helps you set destinations for your growth journey, giving you a clear path for what comes next. Now, let's get into the exercise itself. Follow these steps:

01 Turn to the next page. You will see a circle that represents your comfort zone. Around it, map out areas just beyond your comfort zone (e.g., public speaking, trying a new sport, asking someone out). Then, write a specific goal related to each area.

02 Match that with a Bible verse that gives you courage. There are some options to draw inspiration from on the pages that follow.

03 Each week, choose one area to "explore" by taking that practical step. After each exploration, add it to your comfort zone and reflect on how your map is expanding.

04 Decide on a practical step you can take to move toward that goal.

EQ PRACTICE:
THE COMFORT ZONE CARTOGRAPHER

Things outside your the comfort zone

Area 1 & Goal   Area 2 & Goal

Confort
zone

Area 3 & Goal

As you step into new arenas, let Scripture light your path, offering solace during times of uncertainty and courage in moments of doubt. Allow faith to act as your compass, directing you toward the person you're meant to become.

Turn to the next page for Bible Verses

EQ PRACTICE: THE COMFORT ZONE CARTOGRAPHER

Pairing practical steps with Scripture can give you some extra encouragement and direction. Here are some great examples of Bible verses you can turn to for strength and courage (NIV, 2011/1978):

> "I can do all this through him who gives me strength" (Philippians 4:13).

This verse inspires us to believe in our capabilities, knowing that, with Christ's strength, we can overcome any obstacle.

> "Be strong and courageous. Do not be afraid or terrified because of them, for the Lord your God goes with you; he will never leave you nor forsake you" (Deuteronomy 31:6).

Use this reassuring reminder that God is always by your side to give you the courage to face new challenges.

> "For the Spirit God gave us does not make us timid, but gives us power, love, and self-discipline" (2 Timothy 1:7).

. This verse encourages us to embrace the gifts that God has given us rather than succumb to fear.

> "The Lord is my light and my salvation; whom shall I fear? The Lord is the stronghold of my life; of whom shall I be afraid?" (Psalm 27:1).

Move forward without fear using this beautiful affirmation of God's protection and guidance.

EQ PRACTICE:
THE COMFORT ZONE CARTOGRAPHER

> "But those who hope in the Lord will renew their strength. They will soar on wings like eagles; they will run and not grow weary, they will walk and not be faint" (Isaiah 40:31).

This verse is a reminder that placing your hope in God can renew and sustain your strength, even when times get rough.

> "God is our refuge and strength, an ever-present help in trouble. Therefore, we will not fear, though the earth give way and the mountains fall into the heart of the sea, though its waters roar and foam and the mountains quake with their surging" (Psalm 46:1–3).

These verses assure us that God is our source of strength and protection, no matter what challenges we face.

> "The Lord is my strength and my shield; my heart trusts in him, and he helps me. My heart leaps for joy, and with my song, I praise him" (Psalm 28:7).

This verse beautifully expresses how trusting in God as our strength can lead to joy and praise despite difficult circumstances.

> "So, do not fear, for I am with you; do not be dismayed, for I am your God. I will strengthen you and help you; I will uphold you with my righteous right hand" (Isaiah 41:10).

God promises to support and strengthen us, encouraging us to move forward without fear.

🏃 LET'S BRING IT IN

In this chapter, we've explored how self-doubt can make you feel like you're standing on the edge of a pool, clutching your fears like they're the One Ring. But here's the fun part: Diving into the unknown, armed with courage and faith, turns those jitters into opportunities for growth. Every little step outside your comfort zone adds another badge to your life's adventure vest, prepping you for even bigger quests. Whether it's raising your hand in class or trying out for the basketball team, each leap—even if it feels more like a hop at first—builds your confidence, brick by brick. And while you're creating this epic story, keeping a trusty logbook of bravery helps you track your progress so that you can look back and see just how far you've come.

Along the way, divine guidance becomes your sidekick, whispering encouragement as you face dragons of doubt. You're not alone in this journey; your faith lights the way, giving you the strength to tackle whatever crosses your path. Everyone's courage looks different, and that's perfectly okay. Whether your roar is as loud as a lion's or as timid as a kitten's meow, what matters most is taking action. Celebrate those wins—big or small—and know that embracing challenges with faith and humor is how you'll grow into the amazing person God created you to be.

So, lace up your metaphorical hiking boots, chart new territories, and don't forget that stepping out of your comfort zone isn't about flawless leaps but making that brave first move. Now, you have everything you need to step into God's adventure for your life. Remember, courage isn't the absence of fear—it's the confidence to move forward with God even when you're scared.

Congratulations, you've made it through the obstacle course training! But this isn't the end—it's just the beginning of putting these skills into practice. You've learned how to flip the script on peer pressure, find your way through the digital jungle, honor God in your relationships, and face your fears with faith. At each stage, you've seen that you're not running this race alone. God's got your back, and He's cheering you on every step of the way. It's time to get out there and show the world what a God-powered teen can do!

THIRD QUARTER PRAYER

RELATIONSHIPS AND SOCIAL CHALLENGES

Lord, as I face life's obstacle course, remind me that "For the Spirit God gave us does not make us timid, but gives us power, love, and self-discipline" (NIV, 2011/1978, 2 Timothy 1:7). Thank You for being my spotter when challenges seem too heavy. Give me courage to stand firm in my faith when peer pressure hits hard. Empower me to be a positive influence on my teammates and to choose friends who lift me up in faith. I'm grateful for Your playbook that guides me through tough social situations. Help me navigate relationships with wisdom and integrity, always keeping Your game plan in mind. Let me be a light to others while staying true to Your path. Amen.

PART FOUR
BRINGING IT ALL HOME
(GAME TIME, BABY!)

THE FOURTH QUARTER

BRINGING IT ALL HOME

(GAME TIME, BABY!)

Don't let anyone look down on you because you are young, but set an example for the believers in speech, in conduct, in love, in faith and in purity. –1 Timothy 4:12

CHAPTER 13
GOD'S PLAYBOOK FOR YOUR FUTURE

"For I know the plans I have for you," declares the Lord,
"plans to prosper you and not to harm you,
plans to give you hope and a future."
–Jeremiah 29:11

WE'RE ABOUT to enter the electrifying realm of teen life's fourth quarter, where you'll navigate milestones like preparing for college and a future career. As you stand on the brink of adulthood, this section will take you through the final stretch, turning all of the preparation you've been doing into action. It's kinda like training for the championship game, but instead of just lifting weights, you're also flexing those faith gains. And just as every athlete needs a playbook to hit their stride, you'll find that aligning your spiritual compass with your dreams plays a major role in finding your way through this thrilling but challenging transition.

This chapter explores the art of striking a balance between introspection and ambition, ensuring that you're not just dreaming big but also reflecting deeply. We'll look into how faith can be the lifeline that guides your decisions and strengthens your resilience as you face new beginnings. We'll also discuss mindset practices, emotional assessments, and journaling—techniques that you can add to your toolbox filled with awesome life hacks and use to reveal your God-given talents. Whether it's guidance on using your spiritual gifts or encouragement for embracing the bumps along the road, everything you'll find here aims to kit you out with the wisdom necessary to step confidently into the world that's waiting with open arms.

Unleashing Your Spiritual Superpower

When it comes to life's big game, especially as you prepare for the leap to college and beyond, understanding the plays God has designed just for you can feel like trying to read a cosmic playbook in scribbles. But don't sweat! Your journey begins by discovering how to make the most of the spiritual talents that have been uniquely planted within you. Think back to what you learned in The Second Quarter, where you saw that these are gifts that lift you when nothing else can.

Prayer and Reflection

Unleashing your spiritual superpower starts with faith and introspection. You've figured out what you're the GOAT at and how you can unlock those abilities. Now, you need to determine how you're going to let them guide you going forward. By spending time in prayer and thinking about what impact you'd like to have on the world and how that can align with God's plan for you, you'll slowly start to see the path toward your future illuminated.

Syncing up With God's Guidance

Once you've got a peek at your spiritual toolkit, the next step is recognizing how your personal goals line up with God's divine guidance. It's similar to synchronizing a playlist—you want to make sure all the tunes reflect not only your vibe but also the beats your Creator laid out for you.

Here's a life hack: Keep an open dialogue with God and ask for insights as you set your sights on future achievements. He might answer through Scripture, a nudge in your heart, or the quiet yet unexpectedly profound words of one of your homies. These divine whispers will help you chart a course where your ambitions vibe with His design.

Trusting God's GPS

And then there's embracing trust in God's plan. Gulp, right? It might feel as though you're steering your life's ship with a map only half-inked, trusting that the rest will appear when it needs to, like a Marauder's Map to your destiny. (Okay, I'll stop with the Harry Potter references. Maybe.) Not to mention that transitioning to a new phase in life is often reminiscent of stepping off a cliff and hoping that the clouds will catch you. But remember, God's got a thing for turning these swan dives into epic flights. By leaning into trust, you're allowing faith to turn your fear into anticipation—a much-needed power boost for any teenage superhero on the brink of adulthood.

The Ultimate Compass

Pop quiz: Can you name a famous explorer who ever journeyed without a compass? Exactly! Your faith is basically the same as one of those nifty little devices, except, in this case, it's guiding you beyond what you can see and toward what truly matters. Using your spirituality to inform your planning for your future means keeping your belief front and center in everything you do.

Whether you're deciding on a college major or trying to figure out how you'll contribute to the world's greater good, letting your spirituality guide your decisions guarantees that each turn you take is grounded in something deeper than what feels good at the moment. It's basically like sticking a moral compass onto your first car's dashboard. When challenges arise—and they will—this is what will point you back to the path of integrity and purpose.

So, while the road ahead is as uncertain as a fortune cookie's prediction, let your spiritual compass help you navigate it. Be ready to welcome detours, though; they often lead to unexpected but invaluable life lessons.

In all of this, keep humor in your back pocket. Laughter may not fix problems, but it sure does make dealing with them a lot more bearable. Approach any discoveries with curiosity and an openness to smile at the journey's quirks, knowing that even superheroes sometimes trip over their capes. The college days peeking around the corner will come with high stakes and hefty expectations, but as long as you have God's guidance and your spiritual talents, you'll be well-equipped.

Exercises for Spiritual and Emotional Growth
    When you're in the fourth quarter, it's game time! But before

you go rushing in, let's take a beat to chat about building emotional resilience and spiritual alignment, shall we? First up, there's using mindset practices to pinpoint and apply those fabulous God-given gifts of yours.

The Power of Thinking Positively

Embracing positive thinking is all about treating each challenge as an opportunity, like turning lemons into lemonade or, better yet, divine wine. It's all about capitalizing on what God has given you, and trust me, He doesn't short-change anyone. These gifts aren't just plopped in your lap; they're tools that require discovery and practice—something emphasized in The Second Quarter. So, dive even deeper than before, identify your more subtle passions, and align them with your faith.

Emotional Assessments

The next stop on our journey is emotional assessments. Doing them is similar to taking your spiritual temperature. These assessments help you understand where your feelings wander off to and how they buddy up with your faith. Don't worry, though; they don't require a thermometer. Instead, they involve reflecting on your emotions regularly, maybe using your journal to track your insights. Are they pulling you closer to your beliefs or leading you astray? This introspection allows you to recognize triggers and align your responses, turning those emotional roller coasters into smooth Sunday drives. It's like recalibrating a GPS set to "Faith Road" and ensuring that you're heading in the right direction.

Prayer and Affirmations

Affirmations and prayers are like daily gym sessions for your soul. By bringing them into your routine, you're not just doing some mental bench pressing. It's more like you're flexing spiritual muscles to strengthen your trust in God as your spotter. An affirmation can be as simple as "I am loved" or "With God's guidance, I can overcome anything." Repetition is the secret sauce to this. Place these powerful words around your room, on a mirror, or anywhere they can encourage you with every glance.

Accompany these affirmations with prayer, infusing them with divine strength and consistency to turn wishful thinking into declarations of faith. Combining affirmations and prayer solidifies confidence and fuels your journey with hope and determination. You're not only vocalizing belief but also reinforcing your faith. A powerful prayer, partnered with sincere affirmations, invites peace and purpose into your daily activities.

———

MINDSET PRACTICE: DIVINE TALENT SPOTTER

Reflect on 1 Peter 4:10 for a moment: "Each of you should use whatever gift you have received to serve others" (NIV, 2011/1978).

Now, picture yourself as a sculptor chipping away at marble and unveiling a masterpiece hidden inside. Similarly, with this mindset practice, you can uncover your unique talents and use them to rock the world:

List your top 5 strengths and how they might serve God's purpose.

Visualize using these talents in future scenarios to glorify God.

Practice daily affirmations acknowledging these gifts as God-given.

EQ EXERCISE:
EMOTIONAL COMPASS CHECK

Proverbs 3:5 (NIV, 2011/1978), which states, "Trust in the Lord with all your heart and lean not on your own understanding," is a powerful reminder during this stage of your life. Drawing on this encouragement, respond to the following prompts in your journal:

1. Identify what emotions you experience when you think about the future.

2. Explore how these emotions align with or diverge from faith in God's plan.

3. Practice reframing anxious thoughts into trust-filled prayers.

INTROSPECTIVE JOURNALING
DREAM BIG, PRAY BIGGER

Earlier in the chapter, we spoke about how aligning your goals with God's plans is pretty important, a sentiment expressed in Proverbs 16:3. As this verse says, "Commit to the Lord whatever you do, and he will establish your plans" (NIV, 2011/1978). Set your sights high but always remember to loop in that heavenly perspective. He's got the eagle-eye view, and it beats Google Maps any day.

Now that we've established that intertwining your aspirations with divine insight opens a channel for honest dialogue with God—a relationship nurtured through prayer and promise-filled meditation—ask yourself:

1. How do my current ambitions reflect God's calling for my life?

2. In what ways might God be stretching me beyond my comfort zone?

3. How can I better attune myself to God's guidance in my daily decisions?

LET'S BRING IT IN

You're at the edge of a new chapter in life, but preparing for college and your career is not just about packing up and leaving home. It's also about equipping yourself with faith and introspection. Regardless of what gifts you've been blessed with, view the process of discovering the spiritual talents God has planted within you as an opportunity to connect with something greater than textbooks and tests.

Transitioning to adulthood can feel like trying to predict the plot twists in a blockbuster movie. Expect challenges; you might even face-plant into them a few times, but that's where your humor and faith come into play. When you know that you've got a divine compass leading the way, you can turn each stumble into a chance for laughter. As you set sail onto the waters of college life, let your faith guide your journey. And it's okay to make detours. They often lead you to unexpected lessons and growth. Embrace this adventure with a heart full of excitement, faith, and the knowledge that God's on your side, ready to help you soar.

Now, you're kitted out with your spiritual loadout—talents, direction, and divine backup. Remember, you're not just playing for likes or temporary wins; you're in God's elite squad, ready to make an eternal impact.

CHAPTER 14
COLLEGE GAME PLAN: CHOOSING YOUR ARENA

Whatever you do, work at it with all your heart,
as working for the Lord, not for human masters.
–Colossians 3:23

JUST AS GLADIATORS need a colosseum that suits their skills, you need a college that matches up with your faith and dreams. Choosing where you're going to study isn't just about picking the dopest campus or following your squad—it's about finding a place that feels like home for both your heart and mind. With so many options out there, it's easy to become overwhelmed, like a knight standing in front of a multidimensional portal, unsure which realm holds the key to your destiny. That's where a faith-based approach comes in handy: It's your trusty compass, guiding you through this maze and to the perfect arena for your future adventures.

In this chapter, we're doing a deep dive into the important role your faith can play in selecting the right college. We'll explore how aligning your education with your personal values can lead to a more rewarding experience, and you'll discover tips for navigating campus visits, asking the right questions, and decoding those clever brochures full of smiling students. This journey even involves a little introspective journaling and some emotional decoding, all aimed at helping you find a school where you can thrive both academically and spiritually.

From considering the moral lessons you can find in the curriculum or the spirited community that awaits, you'll learn how to use your beliefs as a lens to evaluate your options. From defining what's truly important to you to understanding what plays a role in shaping your future, get ready to figure out how to align your spiritual strengths with your academic ambitions.

Scouting Report: Finding a College That Vibes With Your Faith

You're a knight about to head off on the legendary quest of choosing a college. Instead of shiny armor, you're donning your faith as your trusty shield. But the mission isn't picking any old castle—uh, college. It's choosing one that feels like home for both you and your beliefs. Why, you ask? Because finding a value-aligned college is like receiving your invitation to Hogwarts, just with less magic and more reasons to strengthen your spiritual journey. (Okay, that was the last one. No more Harry Potter.)

Personal Growth and Development

A college that syncs with your values lets you be you. It's a place where discussing how biblical truths relate to everyday life doesn't raise eyebrows but rather lifts spirits (and possibly grades). When everyone around you gets why Sunday mornings are reserved for worship or knows that the little fish symbol on your backpack is more than a trendy sticker, it reinforces who you are at your core. This environment allows for deep, meaningful conversations that can shape your understanding of the world through the lens of faith. And let's face it, having homies who appreciate your latest corny Christian meme makes everything better.

Academic Success and Satisfaction

No one thrives in an echoey lecture hall where their beliefs feel out of place. Enter the wonder of faith-based colleges: Their coursework often combines knowledge and morality. Can you imagine how awesome it would be to tackle economic inequality not only through graphs and charts but also by discussing ethical perspectives grounded in Scripture? Sign me up!

This intertwining of academics and spirituality does more than boost your grades; it ignites your passion, too. You'll find yourself more motivated because what you're learning resonates deeply with your values, making those late-night study sessions a bit more bearable (even though they're still pretty rough). You see, when what you believe aligns with what you're taught, that's when true academic fulfillment happens.

Community and Belonging

A major perk of these institutions is the passionate community, which creates a sense of belonging that rivals even the most tight-knit youth groups. In a place where shared values aren't just tolerated but celebrated, friendships blossom quicker than sunflower seeds under a summer sun. From campus-wide Bible studies to mission trips that offer you firsthand experiences in serving others, you get to immerse yourself in a network that supports your emotional and spiritual well-being.

These close connections help keep homesickness at bay while propelling you toward becoming a better version of yourself, surrounded by awesome homies and mentors hyping you all the way. Plus, there's always someone around who knows all the words to that obscure worship song you thought only you liked.

Looking Beyond Graduation

Aligning your college choice with faith pays off in the long run, with a ton of career perks coming your way. Many faith-based schools have the benefit of super-strong alumni networks that feel like extended family. These communities do wonders for your job prospects, providing opportunities as well as mentorship from those who've gone before you. You might just find yourself interning at organizations that value the same principles you hold dear and developing skills highly sought after by today's employers, like integrity and self-discipline. This faith-infused education prepares you for professional life without sacrificing the moral compass you've so carefully honed.

Some Helpful Guidelines

So, how do you go about finding this elusive college? Allow me to present a helpful set of guidelines for navigating these hallowed halls:

- Begin your search with institutions known for integrating faith and academics seamlessly.

- Visit campuses when possible, participate in virtual tours if not, and talk to current students about their experiences.
- Ask yourself if the curriculum reflects what you stand for.
- Find out if there are programs that encourage growth in both mind and spirit.

Keeping Your Spiritual Game Strong

So, you're thinking about the big leap into college life, right? This is where you get to choose not just a school or some random classes but really dig deep and pick a major that resonates with your calling. That's where it all starts—finding what gets you hyped rather than just settling for something that'll pay the bills.

Making Major Decisions (Pun Intended)

Now, let's keep it 100. There's more to picking a field of study than signing up for any class because it sounds cool or will lead to a job with a decent salary. Nope! It needs to align with what feels like your purpose, and your faith comes into play here. Imagine waking up every day and being excited to learn because your course connects with who you believe God made you to be.

Think of making decisions about your career as acting out a role only you can nail. It's kind of like performing in a play where the lines are scripted by your values. Choosing a major this way can totally change your college experience from a drag to an adventure.

Crushing Your Courses

Once you've got your field of study down, it's time to figure out how to crush it academically while staying spiritually strong. College can be this whirlwind of late-night study sessions, plans with new friends, and professors tossing assignments at you like confetti. But somewhere in the middle of all this chaos, you need to make sure your faith is on point. How? By prioritizing what matters—God, your spiritual growth, and making those grades shine. It's like juggling flaming torches. But hey, who doesn't love a good challenge?

So, if you're still wondering what path to hack your way through, remember that your faith is this epic GPS guiding you. Align your major with your calling, protect your beliefs fiercely, and keep a check on your emotional compass. No one's saying it'll be easy peasy lemon squeezy, but when you walk this journey with purpose and passion, it's going to be worthwhile. Go out there with your faith intact and eyes set on what truly matters!

———

MINDSET PRACTICE
FAITH-FILTERED COLLEGE LENS

Imagine that you have a pair of glasses that let you see potential colleges through your Christian perspective. Sounds lit, right? Well, that's what this exercise is all about. Before you commit to a school, use this filter to evaluate whether it aligns with your beliefs. Consider what's important to you in a college environment and if that school supports and encourages your faith. Here's how to put your informed decision-making process into practice:

1. *Create a checklist of faith-based criteria for evaluating colleges.*

2. Visualize thriving spiritually at your top college choices.

3. Practice explaining your college choices through a faith perspective.

When you're deciding on a school, you're essentially looking for a place that helps you thrive in both academics and spirituality. When you need inspiration, remember these words from Matthew 6:33: "But seek first his kingdom and his righteousness, and all these things will be given to you as well" (NIV, 2011/1978).

EQ EXERCISE:
MAJOR EMOTIONS DECODER

Have you ever caught yourself feeling stressed about your studies and faith journey colliding? Let Proverbs 19:21 provide comfort with its reminder that "many are the plans in a person's heart, but it is the Lord's purpose that prevails" (NIV, 2011/1978).

In this exercise, you'll decode your emotions around choosing a major and tackling college life. By writing about the prompts in your journal, you'll discover why certain subjects make your heart race with excitement or why others feel like a chore. Once you understand these responses, you can better handle the academic challenges thrown your way and prioritize both personal and spiritual growth.

1. Explore emotions associated with different potential majors.

2. Identify any fears or anxieties about choosing a major and career path.

3. Practice surrendering these emotions to God through prayer.

INTROSPECTIVE JOURNALING

Psalm 25:4 (NIV, 2011/1978) states, **"Show me your ways, Lord, teach me your paths."** Keep these words in mind as you ask yourself the following questions:

How does my choice of college and major align with my understanding of God's purpose for me?

In what ways can I prepare to be a light for Christ on campus?

INTROSPECTIVE JOURNALING

Am I moving toward something meaningful?

How might God use my education to impact His kingdom?

By doing this, you're prepping to be impactful not just in your chosen career but in the broader spectrum of influencing others and spreading positive vibes.

LET'S BRING IT IN

Alright, warriors of wisdom! As you journey through the epic quest of hunting for your perfect college, remember that this chapter is a trusty guide you can return to as often as you need. We've explored how important it is to find a place where faith and academics are as beautifully inseparable as peanut butter and jelly. You've seen that picking a college that vibes with your beliefs isn't just about finding a school; it's about discovering a second home where your spiritual armor is polished daily. Whether it's through deep discussions about morality in economics or seeing classmates nod in understanding during a campus Bible study, this place should support who you are at heart.

Use that faith-filtered college lens to see schools through your Christian specs, making sure that they vibe with what's important to you. And don't forget the power of introspective journaling for aligning learning with purpose. It's the ultimate tool for capturing dreams, doubts, and divine plans while mapping out your path to a passion-filled major.

You've got your game plan locked and loaded. Whether you're heading to a Christian college or stepping into secular territory, you're ready to crush it academically while keeping your faith shield at 100%. Gear up with purpose, passion, and a sprinkle of humor as you step into the unknown. Now, your faith-infused college life awaits, ready to be conquered with courage and conviction.

CHAPTER 15
MONEY MOVES: STEWARDSHIP FOR THE WIN

Honor the Lord with your wealth,
with the firstfruits of all your crops.
–Proverbs 3:9

MANAGING your finances can feel like stumbling through a maze with hidden traps and enticing shortcuts, especially when every shiny thing for sale seems to scream your name. As you explore the world of money moves, picture yourself as the main character in a thrilling adventure game where each financial decision can either lead to new levels of wisdom or set you back into dungeons of debt. This chapter invites you on a journey where you'll discover how smart stewardship and aligning your spending habits with biblical principles can honor God and also set you up for both spiritual fulfillment and financial stability.

Together, we'll unlock the secrets of dodging credit card traps that promise more than they deliver, becoming disciplined in budgeting like a financial ninja, and understanding why slow and steady wins the race when it comes to wealth. You'll gain insights into the art of saving for those unexpected life curveballs, ensuring you're prepared with a safety net rather than clinging to the shaky ropes of impulse buys. We'll also delve into how to identify and avoid quick-fix schemes, focusing instead on building wealth through honest work and perseverance. So, grab your metaphorical toolkit, ready your spreadsheet, and let's transform your understanding of money.

Managing Finances Like a Boss

You're about to buy the latest, greatest gadget because your friend's cousin's neighbor said it's a must-have. Sure, it looks cool, but do you really need it? And can you afford it without swiping the plastic card? Be honest, fam.

This scenario is a good example of the first important lesson in making smart financial decisions that vibe with biblical principles: avoiding the alluring trap of credit card debt.

Swerve the Credit

Handling credit cards can seem like a balancing act on a slippery slope. Swipe here, tap there, and suddenly, you're sitting with a mountain of debt that you didn't even see coming. Proverbs 22:7 hints at this when it says, "The borrower is slave to the lender" (*NIV*, 2011/1978). Basically, this means that loaning money, particularly through credit cards, often ties you down financially, making you serve those monthly statements instead of living freely. Spending within your means helps you swerve this trap. If it sounds kinda lame, think of using discipline to dodge unnecessary expenses as financial ninja training. That should change your perspective!

I'm gonna level with you: Spending money feels good, especially when it's on things that give temporary joy. Maybe it's those crisp sneakers or the latest game everyone's posting about. But when temporary pleasure compromises your financial security, you've got a long-term issue on your hands. I mean, have you ever eaten a whole pizza and felt great for 2.5 seconds before the regret set in? That's what excessive spending can do to your wallet over time.

Savings Will Save You

Savings are super important because they allow you to leap over life's hurdles with greater ease. Imagine if Joseph had just partied through all seven years of plenty. (See Genesis 41:53–42:17 for more on that.) Not so smart, right? Then there's Proverbs 21:20, which mentions that "the wise store up choice food and olive oil, but fools gulp theirs down" (*NIV*, 2011/1978). That's basically an ancient way of saying "save some for later." Building up savings doesn't mean you're stingy; it means you'll be ready when life throws curveballs. Whether it's an unexpected medical bill or fixing that annoying flat tire, having a financial buffer is like having a safety net for when life does you dirty.

Easy Come, Easy Go

Now, let's switch it up and chat about those get-rich-quick scams. You know the ones—the magic beans type of deals. They usually sound too good to be true because they are. Proverbs 13:11 warns us that "dishonest money dwindles away" (*NIV*, 2011/1978). Wealth built through honest work, on the other hand, grows over time. Think of success stories built slowly, brick by brick. These aren't fairy tales—they're examples of diligence and faithfulness paying off. If someone promises you a treasure chest without any effort, it might end up being a treasure map that leads nowhere.

Understanding that slow and steady accumulation works better than rushing after every get-rich-quick trend is vital. The feeling you get when you achieve a goal, knowing that you've put in the work, is incredibly rewarding. It also syncs with God's guidance about prosperity rooted in integrity and honesty.

Making Every Dollar Count

Since we're talking practical skills here, it's essential to manage money like the boss you were born to be. This doesn't just mean keeping track of your income and expenses but also putting your money toward goals and making sure that every dollar counts. Start with creating a simple budget that reflects your values:

1. Grab a journal or open a spreadsheet, jot down your earnings, and outline where your money goes each month.
2. Allocate portions for saving, spending on needs, and yes, even some wants.

Balance is everything. When done right, this approach doesn't restrict you; it empowers you to make informed choices.

Step back, look at the bigger picture, seek God's counsel, and don't rush into decisions that could derail your progress. After all, managing your finances wisely goes beyond numbers; it's a testament to your ability to steward what you've been blessed with in a way that honors both your beliefs and practical needs.

Cultivating Financial Contentment

You're a young guy cruising through life with your trusty skateboard and backpack, trying to juggle everything that teenage life throws at you. But there's one thing most people don't talk about enough, and that's how to develop a healthy mindset around money. Now, before you start zoning out, let's make this interesting —and I promise no boring economics lessons here!

You're Never Too Good to Be Grateful

When you start being thankful for what you've got—your family, friends, that epic gaming console—it changes how you see the world. Instead of focusing on what you don't have, like the latest sneakers that everyone else seems to be rocking, your mind shifts to appreciating your current blessings. This is not just feel-good fluff. It helps you trust that you'll have what you need when you need it because God's got your back. And while it might not instantly land you a vault full of cash, it definitely brings a level of peace and positivity to how you handle money.

Here's a fun exercise: Try the "gratitude blitz." Every night, jot down three things you're thankful for from that day. Maybe it's the way your mom prepared your favorite dinner or a killer round of *Fortnite*. Over time, this practice can build an abundance mindset that can improve your financial decisions, too.

Pick Your Priorities

There's this thing Jesus said in Matthew 6:24 that's pretty straightforward: "No one can serve two masters. Either you will hate the one and love the other, or you will be devoted to the one and despise the other. You cannot serve both God and money" (*NIV*, 2011/1978). It's like trying to ride two skateboards at once—eventually, you'll wipe out.

Focusing on spiritual values rather than getting caught up in material stuff means aligning what you do with what you believe. So, next time you're thinking of spending all your allowance on a flashy new gadget, ask yourself if it supports your values or if it will just give you temporary hype.

Speaking of financial pitfalls, impulse buying is like junk food—fun at the moment, but it leaves you feeling "meh" afterward. And the peer pressure to spend is real, like when all your homies are scoring the latest tech. But here's a cheat code: Think about what matters long term. Would your future self thank you for saving that cash for a killer summer camp or a class trip instead?

Be Intentional

Yes, your task is to make intentional choices about where your resources go, reflecting not just your wants but also wisdom, but that doesn't mean you need to become a frugal hermit. It's more about embodying practical stewardship, taking care of what you have, and making informed decisions.

Here's one straightforward guideline for you: Before any spontaneous purchase, implement a "three-day rule." When you're tempted to buy something, wait three days to decide if you really want it. Chances are, by then, the initial urge will have faded, which often saves you from regret.

Finally, remember that it's all about balance. Enjoy today, plan for tomorrow, but keep focused on what really counts: nurturing your relationship with God, your friends, and your future. Financial stewardship designed from this perspective is less about restrictions and more about freedom—freedom to give, receive, and grow spiritually as well as financially.

———

MINDSET PRACTICE:
ABUNDANCE ATTITUDE SHIFT

Philippians 4:19 states, "And my God will meet all your needs according to the riches of his glory in Christ Jesus" (NIV, 2011/1978). Taking inspiration from this verse, try the following exercise:

List some of the ways that God has provided for you in the past.

Visualize using
your resources
to bless others.

Practice
gratitude for
both
abundance and
scarcity.

EQ EXERCISE: FINANCIAL FEELINGS FINDER

Hebrews 13:5 (NIV, 2011/1978) instructs you to "keep your lives free from the love of money and be content with what you have." With that in mind, let's tackle those feelings that come up when money's the topic:

Identify what emotions are triggered by financial discussions.

Explore the root of any money-related anxieties.

Practice reframing financial challenges as opportunities for growing your faith.

For example, do you get a knot in your stomach when someone talks about finances? Maybe it's anxiety about never having enough or feeling embarrassed because you're not rolling in dough. Although these emotions are totally normal, ignoring them isn't going to help. By recognizing these feelings, you can take control and avoid letting them dictate your choices.

👤 INTROSPECTIVE JOURNALING

Earlier, I mentioned Matthew 6:24, which states that you can't serve both God and money. Now, ask yourself the following questions and journal your thoughts:

How does my approach to money reflect my trust in God's provision?

In what ways can I use my resources to further God's kingdom?

How can I cultivate contentment regardless of my financial situation?

LET'S BRING IT IN

You're now equipped with the mindset to be a financial MVP, making moves that honor God and set you up for success. As we've rolled through this chapter, we've tackled the ups and downs of managing money while keeping your faith front and center. You've seen how living beyond your means can lead to a slippery slope, much like trying to ride a skateboard on ice. Trust me, it's not pretty! We've learned that using credit cards wisely and avoiding impulsive buys are key to financial freedom. Who knew being responsible with cash could be like unleashing your inner financial ninja? Plus, having some savings tucked away means you're ready for life's unexpected plot twists, just like having an extra controller when your main one ghosts you mid-game.

But hey, it's not just about counting pennies and dodging debt. True wealth is about stewarding God's resources like a boss, not just stacking paper. It's also about building an attitude of gratitude. Counting your blessings instead of sneakers could open up new levels of peace and joy in how you handle money. When it comes down to it, making intentional choices—like waiting three days before splurging on that shiny gadget—doesn't make you a buzzkill but shows real wisdom and maturity. So, as you go on your journey to becoming a financial whiz who honors God, remember that balance is everything. Enjoy today, plan for tomorrow, and don't forget to laugh along the way. After all, you've got both the skills and divine guidance to make smart moves without losing sight of what truly matters.

CHAPTER 16
KEEPING IT REAL IN A FAKE WORLD: FAITH IN THE FACE-OFF

Do not conform to the pattern of this world,
but be transformed by the renewing of your mind.
–Romans 12:2

FINDING your Christian crew on campus can be like searching for a rare Pokémon: elusive but so worth the hunt. In a sea of faces and diverse beliefs, discovering those who vibe with your values is vital for both your faith journey and personal growth. Much like choosing the right team members in a video game can make or break your progress, surrounding yourself with homies who share your spiritual groundings can legit turn everyday life into an adventurous expedition where you're not just surviving but thriving. It's about assembling a band of brothers—one that sticks together through victory and defeat and accepts you as you are while propelling you to level up spiritually and personally.

This chapter breaks down the art of finding a squad whose beliefs align with yours and creating a strong network of support that helps you stand firm in your faith. Similar to a gaming tutorial that outlines the strategies and alliances that determine success, this chapter will show you how to nurture these friendships to withstand the world's pressure to fit in. We'll also explore how joining faith-driven communities can reinforce your convictions. Plus, we'll talk about mentors—the wise guides on your spiritual path—and how they can be invaluable in pointing you in the right direction when you're navigating life's uncharted territories.

As you connect with others, you'll discover how keeping it 100 strengthens bonds and why embracing diversity within your Christian community enhances unity without anyone needing to compromise who they are. Covering everything from understanding the significance of actively connecting with fellow believers to celebrating differences and practicing empathy, this chapter is a road map for growing in faith and authenticity, and it's here to make sure that you stay true to yourself despite the ever-present call to conformity.

Finding Your Christian Crew on Campus

It's so important to move through life with the right squad, one that accepts you for who you are and pushes you to level up on the daily. But in today's world, finding friends who resonate with your values is like discovering a rare power-up in a video game. And just like choosing toxic teammates can lead to disaster in gaming, choosing the wrong crew off-screen can derail your journey toward personal growth and faith development.

Choosing Your Starting Lineup in Life

Let's say you're playing an intense multiplayer game online, and despite your mad skills, you're struggling. Then, you sync up with that one teammate who shares your play style and strategy. Suddenly, victory is within your grasp! Similarly, aligning yourself with homies who are strong in their faith can boost your spiritual growth like no cheat code ever could. And sure, hanging out with peeps who mirror your values can lead to fun, but it's more about building a supportive network. They become outlets where you can discuss challenges, celebrate wins, and find encouragement when the struggle is real.

The importance of surrounding yourself with like-minded individuals goes beyond just social preference. It's a shield when facing the pressure of conformity. In the same way that joining gaming clans keeps your tactics sharp, immersing yourself in study groups focused on Christian beliefs can reinforce the boundaries you've set for yourself. Your friends' positive behavior will rub off on you, inspiring alignment between your daily actions and core values. This influence isn't accidental; it's a matter of design, just like customizing your avatar to match your gaming skills.

NPCs Can Be MVPs

You know those NPCs in games who give sage advice? They're not just there for decoration! In real life, mentors play similar roles. Getting guidance from someone further along on their spiritual journey can be invaluable. A mentor is like a beacon helping you maintain your focus and direction in uncharted territory. These guides offer wisdom tailored to your personal experiences, making them key players in bolstering your faith.

Making an effort to connect with these homies on the regular supports both the group dynamics and your individual journeys. Much like practicing repeatedly leads to mastering a difficult level, nurturing these relationships improves mutual growth and understanding. So, whether it's attending youth meetups or volunteering at church events, throw yourself into activities that strengthen your community ties.

Keeping It 100

Open communication is the glue that holds everything together. Keeping it 100 builds trust and encourages honesty among your bros. When ideas clash or things get heated, discuss them openly. You'll be amazed at how much smoother your interactions become when everyone's on the same page.

While building this friendship fortress, remember to practice empathy. Be mindful of others' perspectives and emotions, just as you'd want them to be considerate of yours. This mindset encourages an environment filled with understanding and nurtures connections.

Finding Your Tribe

Now, don't think all this means you need to be surrounded purely by these saint-like people who are seemingly immune to making mistakes. Nah, fam! Even within a solid Christian community, you'll find all kinds of struggles and wins. Embracing these differences and respecting diversity promotes unity, strengthens your bonds, and makes a vibrant community even more lit. Think of it as assembling a team with various skill sets needed for a quest —each person brings something invaluable to the table.

So, the guidelines for finding your Christian crew are pretty straightforward: look for like-minded peeps, do stuff together that you all vibe with, keep it 100 through open communication, and emphasize empathy and diversity. This approach will empower you to continue growing in faith while staying true to yourself.

Authenticity All-Star: Being the Real You in a World of Posers

These days, standing out sometimes feels like trying to spot Waldo at a red-and-white-striped convention. There's such an overwhelming pressure from society to fit in, to blend into the crowd, and to conform to what is considered "normal." Let's be real, though: The true adventure begins when you decide not to be a clone of everyone else but to channel your faith and maintain your authenticity.

Swerving Societal Pressure

Swerving societal pressure is all about embracing the unique version of yourself that your faith helps you see. Society loves a good cookie cutter, but true fulfillment comes when you ditch the mold and bake your own quirky shape. Recognizing that God has set you apart for something special is a personal transformation that allows you to grow beyond the box other people keep trying to stuff you into.

Now, you might be wondering, *How do I even begin to align my actions with my beliefs?* I'm so glad that you asked! Think about this: Every time you make a decision, big or small, you're casting a vote for who you want to become. When you're scrolling through social media, yeet the urge to hit the "like" button just because everyone else is doing it. Be intentional about what vibes with your beliefs and values. Maybe skip those TikToks that make you feel some type of way—after all, you wouldn't willingly dive into murky water without checking what lies beneath, would you?

Peer pressure can turn any chill session into a dance with conformity, but here's the tea: You have the power to change the music. Every day hands you multiple opportunities where you'll need to stand firm in your decisions. Whether choosing how to react to a meme or deciding whether to hop onto the latest trend, these choices reflect your inner compass. Make sure the needle points to a place you're proud of. After all, standing firm is less about what you say and more about what you do when no one's watching.

Be You-Nique

Flexing your uniqueness isn't just about being different for the sake of it; it's about echoing the masterpiece you are in God's eyes. In a world obsessed with blending in, standing out can be a beacon of inspiration. Just like Jesus preached love and acceptance in the face of criticism, embracing the qualities that make you different rather than seeking approval from worldly standards is fulfilling God's vision for you.

Maintaining authenticity doesn't mean taking yourself too seriously, though. Humor is a fantastic resource on this journey; I keep bringing it up for a reason. Life as a Christian teenager is like a hilarious sitcom, complete with comic relief moments. Laugh at your quirks, embrace the awkwardness of discovering who you truly are, and don't forget to find joy even in the flops. Faith teaches us that there's room for grace and growth, so why not giggle along the way?

Think of your authentic self as a brand. But this isn't about marketing as much as it's about owning your identity. Your faith acts as both a guiding star and a lens through which you view the world. Filter your experiences through the truths that really matter to you. Before making decisions, ask yourself: *Does this bring me closer to my genuine self, or am I putting up a front for someone else?*

Here's where faith flexes its muscle: It fuels resilience against the tug-of-war between wanting to belong and staying true to yourself. Take that leap of faith and trust God's plan despite not knowing every twist and turn ahead.

Finding Your Way

Navigating social circles can be tricky, like trying not to spill your drink while holding too many things at a party. But let's be honest—even if you end up with a stain, it's nothing a bit of deter-gent and laughter can't fix. Remember, the people who matter will appreciate the unfiltered version of you. Stand firm in your unique values at meetups or hangouts because being authentic often inspires others to do the same.

So, here's the scoop: maintaining authenticity through faith requires a beautiful balance of courage, trust, and a sprinkle of humor. Resist fitting into societal molds, stay true to the unique path God has crafted for you, and don't shy away from expressing the gifts you've been given. Align your actions with your beliefs, trusting that the strength of your convictions will serve as both shield and guide.

———

EQ EXERCISE:
FAITH—FEELINGS SYNC

"Above all else, guard your heart, for everything you do flows from it." The following exercise is inspired by these words from Proverbs 4:23 (NIV, 2011/1978). In your journal, respond to the following prompts, taking your time to really engage with each one:

Identify what emotions you experience when living out your faith.

Explore any disconnect between your beliefs and actions.

Practice aligning your emotional responses with your faith values.

MINDSET PRACTICE:
AUTHENTICITY AMPLIFIER

Psalm 139:13 is a reminder of how purposely God has designed each of us, stating: **"For you created my inmost being; you knit me together in my mother's womb"** (NIV, 2011/1978). With this in mind, complete the following exercise:

List the unique qualities that God has given you.

Visualize confidently expressing your faith in challenging situations.

Practice affirming your identity in Christ daily.

INTROSPECTIVE JOURNALING

Matthew 5:16 says, "Let your light shine before others, that they may see your good deeds and glorify your Father in heaven" (NIV, 2011/1978). Reflect on this verse for a moment, then respond to the following questions in your journal:

In what areas of my life do I struggle to live authentically for Christ?

How can I better integrate my faith into my daily routines and decisions?

What steps can I take to strengthen my faith to prepare for challenges?

LET'S BRING IT IN

Venturing further into the realm of friendship and authenticity is like playing a co-op game where your team dynamics ultimately determine whether you win or lose. We've explored how surrounding yourself with a Christian crew can be your secret weapon against the societal pressure to conform. You've also seen that choosing the right homies is like assembling an elite squad in your favorite multiplayer game: Everyone plays their part, and together, you level up in life and faith.

But let's not forget the power of standing out and embracing the quirks that make you unique. Society may keep pressing "copy and paste," but you've got a colorful palette to paint your own masterpiece. God designed you with a specific purpose, so play the game your way, dodge conformity traps, and inspire others with your originality.

We've also seen how authenticity isn't just about being different; it's about being real in a world of filters and edits. With faith as your compass, think of each decision as a vote for the person you're becoming. Whether sharing a meme that echoes your beliefs or choosing silence in the face of chaos, these actions are your signatures on God's plan for you. And don't worry about tripping over life's bumps; after all, every superhero story has its bloopers. Laugh at the awkwardness, dance to your own tune, and remember —maintaining your uniqueness is not only courageous but contagious. So, go ahead, channel your faith, and celebrate the wonderful, one-of-a-kind journey that lies ahead.

CHAPTER 17
FINDING YOUR GROOVE – ALIGNING YOUR ACTIONS WITH YOUR BELIEFS

Do not merely listen to the word, and so deceive yourselves.
Do what it says.
–James 1:22

FINDING your groove is like finding the beat in a song—when you hit it, everything starts to come together, and you're suddenly moving through life like it's the latest TikTok dance trend. Soon, you'll be strolling down the hallways of your high school as if it's a concert stage, feeling entirely in sync with who you are and what you believe.

Now, how do you reach that sweet spot where your actions truly reflect your inner values? That's the million-dollar question that this chapter hopes to answer with stories and life hacks that promise to help you step into your own rhythm without tripping over those proverbial shoelaces. It's all about letting go of the struggle between what you say you believe and how you actually live. There's no need for OTT dance moves or grand gestures—just simple, swift steps toward aligning your daily deeds with your true beliefs.

Throughout this awesome chapter, you'll explore valuable techniques and exercises designed to bring clarity and purpose to the seemingly boring parts of your life. You'll learn how to use something as basic as a notebook to turn everyday routines into meaningful spiritual expressions. You'll also uncover the magic behind stress-busting methods that turn chaos into calm. Plus, get ready to cruise through challenges with courage and thrive with community support from church groups and faith-based meetings.

When obstacles arise, there'll be no need to worry—you'll also find insights on transforming stumbles into strides toward genuine living. It's all about creating harmony between your beliefs and actions, keeping life's melody flowing smoothly and naturally without missing a beat.

Practical Strategies for Living Out Your Faith Daily

If you often find yourself waking up and starting your day with a groggy mind, maybe the next time it happens, before reaching for that double espresso or endlessly scrolling through social media, hit pause. Take a deep breath, clear your head, and dive into a simple morning prayer or a few minutes of mindfulness. This new routine might seem minor at first glance, but it's a super powerful way to start embedding faith into your everyday life.

Prayer and Mindfulness

Developing a consistent practice of prayer and mindfulness can be the cornerstone of incorporating faith throughout your day. Here's why:

- Prayer is like having an open line with God—no Wi-Fi needed—and taking a moment to express gratitude or ask for guidance can set a positive tone for the whole day.
- Mindfulness, on the other hand, allows you to stay present and aware, creating a mindset that aligns with your spiritual beliefs.

Whether it's during a bus ride to school or while getting ready for bed, finding little windows for these practices helps bridge the gap between what you believe and how you live daily.

Little by Little

Okay, so you've decided to lay down some habits that reflect Christian values—kindness, patience, generosity. But real talk, some days, being patient feels as challenging as solving a Rubik's Cube blindfolded. Even when it's hard, every opportunity you take to practice these virtues brings you a little bit closer to aligning your actions with your beliefs. The main thing is consistency. Maybe it's offering a listening ear to a friend who's had a rough day, lending a hand to someone in need without expecting anything in return, or choosing to smile at strangers. Over time, these actions become natural extensions of your faith.

Becoming an active member of a community church can do wonders for leveling up your faith and encouraging growth. It's there that you'll find a group of unique peeps, each on their own journey, coming together to share, learn, and support each other.

Attending services, volunteering for church activities, or joining youth groups strengthens your spiritual foundation and also gives you a nurturing environment where faith becomes communal. This sense of belonging and shared purpose can be a great motivating force to keep you vibing with your beliefs even when times get tough.

Clocking and Crushing Obstacles

Speaking of challenges, ever feel like every step forward comes with its own set of roadblocks? Being able to clock and then crush obstacles that hold you back from living your best Christian life is a must if you want to build resilience. When you're confronted with these hurdles—maybe in the form of peer pressure, doubts, or temptations—remember that overcoming them isn't about bull-dozing through with sheer determination; it's about switching things up and growing stronger with each experience.

Seek guidance from mentors, participate in discussions, or lean on faith-based literature to gain wisdom and perspective. Embrace these struggles as opportunities to deepen your understanding and strengthen your resolve. This will ultimately allow you to live more authentically according to your beliefs.

As you blend faith into everyday life, you'll begin to notice subtle shifts—a greater sense of peace, an increase in compassion, a deeper connection with others, and a clearer path forward. Your daily actions will start to mirror your beliefs, and soon enough, they'll become second nature.

Exercises and Techniques for Spiritual Growth

In a world where balancing belief and action often feels like an endless uphill battle, finding your groove can sometimes feel as impossible as catching smoke with your bare hands. But don't sweat it! I've got some life hacks to help sync up those daily steps with your spiritual talk and create a harmonious rhythm in your life.

Chores With a Purpose

Now, you might wonder how simple chores could possibly become significant expressions of faith. Well, think about it. When you jot down what you need to do in your journal, you're not just documenting tasks; you're capturing the essence of gratitude, mindfulness, and intention. It's about embracing each moment as an opportunity to live aligned with what you believe. This practice not only enhances spiritual growth but also makes the mundane feel like part of a grander purpose. So, grab a notebook—or start typing on your phone—and begin turning your day-to-day life into a faith-filled parade!

Life Hacks to Stress Less

Stress-free days make room for more meaningful connections between your actions and beliefs. They help unravel knots of tension, allowing your heart and mind to be open and receptive to spiritual growth. So, to help keep that path serene and clear, let's dive into some simple stress-reduction techniques.

Imagine stress as an uninvited guest at your peace party—one you can gently nudge out the door with easy activities like deep breathing, taking a quick walk, or even belting out your favorite song in the shower. These acts might seem small, but they carry the big power of helping you maintain a peaceful mind (Kriakous et al., 2021).

Very Mindful

Mindfulness plays a starring role here, too! Connecting your thoughts to the present moment without judgment creates a rewarding environment for growth. It's like giving your brain a warm hug, reminding it that everything's okay, and keeping the chaos at bay (Shapiro et al., 2006). Blending prayer, mindfulness, and self-awareness into your routine—even during a quick lunchtime break—encourages a serene spirit and opens doors to deeper understanding. These practices shine a light on the clearer paths toward living in alignment with your values.

Review and Reflect

But what if you trip on this path? Don't sweat it! Part of the journey involves stumbling, learning, and getting back up stronger. Here's where ongoing evaluation becomes your best buddy. Think of it as your very own review board that checks in every now and then to see how things are going.

For example, are your current challenges making you grow, or have they turned into old, comfy slippers, trapping you in stagnation? Adjusting your goals to match your evolving self is important because it ensures the continual growth and strengthening of your faith. It's basically like transitioning from beginner mode to a seasoned player in your favorite video game.

As you evaluate your progress, take time to reflect on how your exercises—whether it's journaling, stress-busting techniques, mindfulness practices, or a combination—are influencing your life. Are you seeing changes in your attitude, your relationships, or your resilience against life's hiccups? These reflections will give you valuable insights that show you where you need to make adjustments. After all, we're aiming for a life where belief and action dance seamlessly together to create a symphony of authentic living.

———

MINDSET PRACTICE
THE DAILY POWER-UP CHALLENGE

Colossians 3:23 (NIV, 2011/1978), which states, "Whatever you do, work at it with all your heart, as working for the Lord, not for human masters," perfectly captures the mindset of turning every daily action into an act of worship. This verse can help you understand that living out your faith isn't just about church stuff but about approaching everything with a God-focused attitude. It's about turning mundane habits into power-charged opportunities for expressing your Christian values.

Are you ready to turn your everyday routine into a spiritual power move? This exercise is like creating your personal faith highlight reel, but instead of just watching replays, you're the main player in God's game plan! Follow these steps:

1. Divide a page in your journal into daily segments.
2. Each week, list three routine activities that you'll turn into opportunities for expressing your faith.
3. Write a statement on how you will put those ideas into action.
4. End each day by rating how you turned those actions into God-honoring moments.
5. Review your progress weekly and level up your challenges. You might want to have a dedicated journal for repeating this exercise.

MINDSET PRACTICE
THE DAILY POWER-UP CHALLENGE

When you start treating every moment as game time with God, you'll start seeing your daily routine as epic side quests in your faith journey!

INTROSPECTIVE JOURNALING

Psalm 139:23 (NIV, 2011/1978) says, "Search me, God, and know my heart; test me and know my anxious thoughts." This encourages honest self-reflection and openness with God. So, it's time for some real talk with the Big Guy upstairs! Journal your responses to these deep-reflection questions:

When did your actions today match up with your faith, and when did they miss the mark?

What's holding you back from living out your faith more boldly?

How can you turn tomorrow's challenges into opportunities to show God's love?

For each entry, include
- daily faith victories and struggles
- prayer requests and answered prayers
- questions you're wrestling with
- goals for growing your faith game

🏃 LET'S BRING IT IN

As you journey through life, syncing your spiritual talk with your daily walk might feel a bit like trying to teach a cat to do tricks—challenging but oh-so-rewarding. This chapter has been all about finding ways to blend those beliefs into the everyday grind. From squeezing in prayer and mindfulness during a morning stretch to turning chores into moments to express gratitude, you're not just going through the motions; you're creating a day that's filled with meaningful actions that mirror what really matters to you. Throw in a few stress-busting techniques and some reflective journaling, and suddenly, what seemed impossible becomes a fun adventure of living out your faith.

Stumbling is part of the gig, though! But with ongoing evaluation and a sprinkle of kindness toward yourself, each trip-up becomes a step toward greater growth. Connecting with your community and getting involved in church activities can make all the difference, creating bonds that strengthen your resolve when resistance hits hard. Through patience, kindness, and a touch of humor, these practices become more than tasks—they turn into effortless extensions of who you are and what you believe. So, go ahead, let your life groove to the rhythm of faith, and continue on this grand adventure of aligning belief with action.

Congratulations, you've made it through the fourth-quarter playbook! You're now kitted out with God's game plan for crushing college, your career, and life's biggest challenges. You're not just leveling up for yourself, though. You're part of God's ultimate team, making moves that matter for eternity. Stay connected to your divine coach, keep your spiritual squad close, and never forget that, with God as your guide, you're already on the winning team. Now, get out there and show the world what you're made of!

FOURTH QUARTER PRAYER

FUTURE PREPARATION

Divine Lord, as I prepare for the next level of the game, I trust Your words: "For I know the plans I have for you, plans to prosper you and not to harm you, plans to give you hope and a future" (NIV, 2011/1978, Jeremiah 29:11). Thank You for going ahead of me to prepare my path. Give me wisdom to make choices that honor You as I plan for college and my career.

Empower me to face new challenges with faith and confidence. I'm grateful for Your guidance in every decision. Help me stay focused on Your game plan when distractions come. Let me remember that with You as my Coach, I'm qualified for whatever position You've called me to play.

Amen.

AFTERWORD

As we wrap up this journey, let's kick back and reflect on what we've dived into. We've spent a good amount of time talking about who the real MVP in our lives is: God. Understanding His unconditional love is a game-changer. It's like having an all-season pass to security and purpose. The more you lean into this relationship, the more you'll find yourself standing firm even when life tries to tackle you with challenges.

By now, you've mastered the art of using the Bible not as some boring old instruction manual but as your personal playbook. It's full of strategies for decision-making and personal growth. The more you engage with it, the more you'll start seeing it as that wise friend who always knows what to say. And let's not forget prayer, the spiritual fuel that keeps you running smoothly no matter what roadblocks you hit. It's your direct line to the creator of the universe—a pretty awesome hotline if you ask me. Through all those quiet talks with God, you've probably noticed a dip in anxiety and a surge in peace.

Next, we tackled finding your position on God's team. You've discovered unique strengths and realized that they aren't just happy accidents—they're gifts from God. Whether you're a natural leader or someone who excels at behind-the-scenes work, these talents are meant to be shared. Learning to embrace them and use them for service makes playing on God's team incredibly rewarding.

You've seen the importance of role models, too. They're like the highlight reels of faith, showing you what's possible when someone lives authentically. Their stories can inspire you to rise to the occasion and do more than you ever thought possible.

Now, stepping out onto life's playing field, you're equipped like never before. You've started learning how to navigate challenges with a spirit connected to God, impacting the world around you one day at a time. You've become a light in the world, which is part of your life's grand adventure—no capes required. But hey, nobody's perfect. You're learning to leverage your strengths while working on those weak spots. It's all part of the growth process. Every superstar started somewhere, and the same goes for you.

Tackling life's challenges head-on, especially during these teenage years, can feel like an obstacle course from the Olympics. But guess what? You've got new strategies up your sleeve to resist peer pressure and surround yourself with positive influences. You're figuring out how to handle social media like a pro and have started maintaining a healthy digital balance without losing yourself in the noise. We've also talked about dating. Building God-honoring relationships might seem tricky, especially when romantic love comes into play, but you've gained insights on navigating this path with wisdom. It's about growing with someone while keeping your values front and center.

You're dreaming big and praying bigger, aligning your goals with a higher plan—it's like having a personal trainer for your soul. As you approach things like college and career choices, you're building a faith-based approach that'll make these decisions feel less daunting and more fulfilling. From choosing a major to tackling finances with biblical wisdom, you're setting the groundwork for a generous, purposeful life.

You might feel like you're stepping onto a new playing field, the likes of which you've never seen before. But that just means you've leveled up. Preparing for your 20s and beyond feels epic, doesn't it? This is where everything comes together. Your talents and interests align with God's plan, and, with His input, you get to create a road map uniquely yours.

In the end, remember this: Life's a lot like a grand game. It has its ups, downs, and unexpected twists. But rooted in faith and strengthened by community, you've been given tools to play it well. Always remember that God's cheering you on from the sidelines, ready to guide you through each new chapter. Now, go out there and live your story with humor, heart, and purpose—and have fun doing it!

———

ABOUT THE AUTHOR

Nathaniel Bennett is a devoted husband, father, and Christian author dedicated to helping young people discover their God-given purpose. With a heart for youth ministry and a passion for translating timeless biblical wisdom into contemporary guidance, Bennett is a trusted voice for families navigating life's challenges through faith.

Drawing from his experiences raising sons in today's world, Bennett understands the unique pressures facing modern teens and their parents. When he's not writing, he enjoys coaching youth sports and mentoring in his community. Through the *God's Game Plan* series, Bennett combines motivational wisdom and scientific research with biblical principles to help the next generation live out their divine purpose with courage and authenticity.

———

Pay It Forward

Drop Your Review, Change the Game

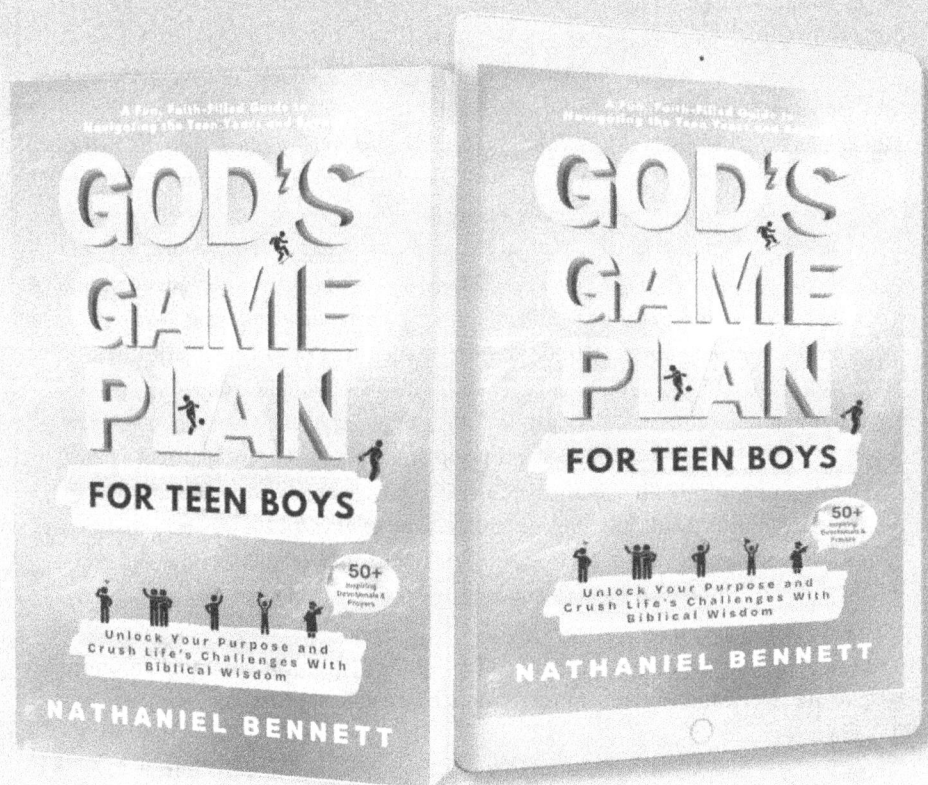

Leave a ★★★★★ review for
God's Game Plan for Teen Boys.
Your assist will help another teen win at faith.

BIBLIOGRAPHY

Aaron. (2024, September 2). *Mastering social skills: The key to effective interpersonal communication*. Leader Navigation. https://www.leadernavigation.com/social-skills-3/

Abimbola, E. (2024, April). *Understanding resilience from a biblical perspective*. iBelieve. https://www.ibelieve.com/christian-living/understanding-resilience-from-a-biblical-perspective.html

Adolescent Psychiatry Staff. (2021, July 22). *Teen stress: Biggest triggers & 7 ways to cope*. Society for Adolescent Psychiatry. https://www.adolescent-psychiatry.org/teen-stress-biggest-triggers-ways-to-cope/

Alale, E. (2022, February 18). *The importance of mentorship to spiritual maturity*. Bethel Campus Fellowship. https://www.bethelcampusfellowship.com/the-importance-of-mentorship-to-spiritual-maturity

Arnold, M. B. (2014). *Where am I? How to discover and develop your spiritual gifts and talents*. The Church of Jesus Christ Latter-Day Saints. https://www.churchofjesuschrist.org/study/liahona/2014/12/youth/where-am-i?lang=eng

Benefits of community service. (2018). Western Connecticut State University. https://www.wcsu.edu/community-engagement/benefits-of-volunteering/

Beyond Happiness Team. (2024, July 16). *Attracting wealth with a spiritual mindset: A holistic approach to prosperity*. Beyond Happiness. https://beyondhappiness.love/attracting-wealth-with-a-spiritual-mindset-a-holistic-approach-to-prosperity/

BibleStudyTools Staff. (20224, November 5). *15 amazing attributes of God: What they mean and why they matter*. Bible Study Tools. https://www.biblestudytools.com/bible-study/topical-studies/15-amazing-attributes-of-god-what-they-mean-and-why-they-matter.html

Biblical principles for managing finances. (2024, July 1). Impact Family Christian Counseling Network. https://impact.vision/blog/biblical-principles-for-managing-finances/

Birt, J. (2023, July 31). *24 reasons why mentorship is important*. Indeed Career Guide. https://www.indeed.com/career-advice/career-development/why-is-a-mentor-important

Boa, K. (2022, April 4). *Using your time wisely*. Reflections Ministries. https://reflections.org/using-your-time-wisely/

Boniwell, I., & Tunariu, A. D. (2019). *Positive psychology: Theory, research, and applications*. Open University Press.

Carroll, A. (2021). *What kind of woman does God approve of?* Proverbs 31 Ministries.

https://proverbs31.org/read/devotions/full-post/2021/03/12/what-kind-of-woman-does-god-approve-of

Center for Children and Youth. (2025, January 10). *10 mental health activities for teens.* https://ccy.jfcs.org/mental-health-activities-for-teens/

Ciampi, R. C. (2021, April 12). *Resiliency, perseverance, and integrity.* Robert C. Ciampi, LCSW, PSYA. https://www.rciampi.com/blog/281853-resiliency-perseverance-and-integrity

CityRise. (2024, January 23). *Why community is essential for personal and spiritual growth.* CityRise Church. https://cityrise.org/blog/2024/01/23/why-community-is-essential-for-personal-and-spiritual-growth

Confucius. (n.d.). *Confucius quotes.* BrainyQuote. https://www.brainyquote.com/quotes/confucius_101164

Datu, J. A. D., & Fincham, F. D. (2024). *Development and preliminary validation of the Divine Connectedness Scale in the USA. Journal of Religion and Health, 63*(5), 3862-3877. https://doi.org/10.1007/s10943-024-02111-7

Davtian, M. (2023, July 10). *The dark side of the "abundance mindset."* Seek With Ser. https://www.seekwithser.com/post/demystifying-the-abundance-mindset-the-opposite-of-abundance-is-not-scarcity-its-greed

Duckworth, A. (2016). *Grit: The power of passion and perseverance.* Scribner.

Dunne, K. (2022). *Personal SWOT analysis.* Mindtools. https://www.mindtools.com/aaiakpy/personal-swot-analysis

Edison, T. (n.d.). *Thomas A. Edison quotes.* BrainyQuote. https://www.brainyquote.com/quotes/thomas_a_edison_132683

Faith on View Christian College. (2024, January 2). *Unlocking reasons: Why choose a faith-based college?* Faith on View. https://www.faithonview.com/unlocking-reasons-why-choose-a-faith-based-college/

Fan, R. (2019, February 18). *Life doesn't get easier, we just get stronger.* The Odyssey Online. https://www.theodysseyonline.com/life-doesnt-get-easier-we-just-get-stronger

15 Amazing Attributes of God: What They Mean and Why They Matter. (2019, August 17). Bible Study Tools; Salem Web Network. https://www.biblestudytools.com/bible-study/topical-studies/15-amazing-attributes-of-god-what-they-mean-and-why-they-matter.html

Foster, L. (2024, March 25). *How should Christians think through career choices?* Australian Christian College. https://www.acc.edu.au/blog/how-should-christian-think-through-career-choice/

Gilham, P. (2020). The apostle Paul's secret to resilience: Embracing trials through faith and scripture. *Lifetime Ministries.* https://www.lifetime.org/the-apostle-pauls-secret-to-resilience-embracing-trials-through-faith-and-scripture

How does social media affect mental health? Understanding the impact and finding balance. (2024, July 31). Take Root Therapy. https://www.losangelesmftherapist.com/

post/how-does-social-media-affect-mental-health-understanding-the-impact-and-finding-balance/

How therapy promotes emotional resilience in adolescents. (2025, February 17). New Horizons Recovery Centers. https://www.newhorizonscenters.com/blog/how-therapy-promotes-emotional-resilience-in-adolescents

How to choose a career that aligns with my personal values. (n.d.). Colorado Christian University. https://www.ccu.edu/blogs/cags/2018/08/how-to-choose-a-career-that-aligns-with-my-personal-values/

How to handle peer pressure. (2024, February 7). Sedona Sky Academy. https://www.sedonasky.org/blog/how-to-handle-peer-pressure

Howard-Snyder, D., & McKaughan, D. J. (2022, January 8). Faith and resilience. *International Journal for Philosophy of Religion*, *91*, 205–241. https://doi.org/10.1007/s11153-021-09820-z

Inside ICON. (2024). *Creating a personal development plan for career advancement*. ICON. https://careers.iconplc.com/blogs/2024-10/creating-a-personal-development-plan-for-career-advancement

Integrity in worship. (n.d.). Bible Hub. https://biblehub.com/topical/i/integrity_in_worship.htm

James 2:17 Study Bible: Even so faith, if it has no works, is dead in itself. (2025). Biblehub.com. https://biblehub.com/study/james/2-17.htm

Janette. (2017). *10 financial principles that are biblical*. Back to the Bible. https://www.backtothebible.org/post/10-financial-principles-that-are-biblical

Journaling to increase self-awareness. (n.d.). Prosper. https://prosper.liverpool.ac.uk/postdoc-resources/reflect/journaling-to-increase-self-awareness/

Kuhrt, J. (2014, August 9). *How should our faith affect the way we live?* Grace + Truth. https://gracetruth.blog/2014/08/09/how-should-our-faith-affect-the-way-we-live/

Lewis, C. S. (n.d.). *C. S. Lewis quotes*. Goodreads. https://www.goodreads.com/quotes/8188266-hardships-often-prepare-ordinary-people-for-an-extraordinary-destiny

Lindsey, T. (2021, August 4). *Week 02: Discover your design*. Seacoast Church. https://grow.seacoast.org/virtualinsidetrack/lesson-02/

Marboli, S. (n.d.). *Steve Marboli quote*. #PassItOn. https://www.passiton.com/inspirational-quotes/8314-life-doesn-t-get-easier-or-more-forgiving-we

Mattingley, R. (2024, August 21). *Planning your career with Christian values: A comprehensive guide*. Share the Struggle. https://www.sharethestruggle.org/blog/christian-career-guidance

McLean Hospital. (2024, March 29). *The social dilemma: Social media and your mental health*. https://www.mcleanhospital.org/essential/it-or-not-social-medias-affecting-your-mental-health

Milkop, A. (2022). *A letter to your future self.* Antonia Milkop. https://antoniamilkop.com/2022/01/01/a-letter-to-your-future-self/

Moon, S. (2024, March 3). *Navigating cultural diversity: A biblical journey into embracing the third culture.* Mosaics. https://nextg.org/navigating-cultural-diversity-a-biblical-journey-into-embracing-the-third-culture/

Moore, M. (2024, May 8). *Financial literacy for teens made easy: Money skills management for building your credit score, budgeting essentials, and college savings, even with limited income for financial independence.* Self-published.

Morris, C. (2007, June 5). *Impacting the workplace for Christ.* C.S. Lewis Institute. https://www.cslewisinstitute.org/resources/impacting-the-workplace-for-christ/

Neenan, M. (2018). *Cognitive behavioural coaching: Distinctive features.* Routledge.

New International Version. (2011). BibleGateway.com. Original publication 1978 https://www.biblegateway.com/versions/New-International-Version-NIV-Bible/

Nicole, A. (2018, January 29). *Sacred journaling practices.* A Soulful Rebellion. https://asoulfulrebellion.com/blog/the-therapeutic-art-of-journaling

Niranjan, D. (2024, May 17). *Bible verses about trusting God in difficult times in 2025.* Divine Disclosures. https://www.divinedisclosures.com/bible-verses-about-trusting-god/

O'Neill, A. (2025). *The importance of mentorship (and what to look for in a mentor).* Trochia. https://trochia.org/the-importance-of-mentorship-and-what-to-be-look-for-in-a-mentor/

Odebode, I. (2022, February 18). *The importance of mentorship to spiritual maturity.* Bethel Campus Fellowship. https://www.bethelcampusfellowship.com/the-importance-of-mentorship-to-spiritual-maturity

Pemberton, C. (2015). *Resilience: A practical guide for coaches.* Open University Press.

Perry, E. (2022, February 11). *8 ways to overcome self-doubt once and for all.* Betterup. https://www.betterup.com/blog/overcoming-self-doubt

Po, J. (2023, April 7). *Building a foundation of faith: Perceiving subjective truth through a relationship with God.* Medium. https://medium.com/@johnpo357/building-a-foundation-of-faith-perceiving-subjective-truth-through-a-relationship-with-god-1667723ad9b2

Ramirez, S. (2024, November 18). *How to write an achievable 5-year plan that works for you.* BetterUp. https://www.betterup.com/blog/5-year-plan

Ream, S. (2022, November 1). *Cultivating Christian community.* A Woman Created on Purpose. https://www.awomancreatedonpurpose.com/news/community

Reeves, A. (2024, August 8). *Universe manifestation prayer: 11 prayers for abundance.* Business & Marketing Coach for Service Providers. https://alisonreeves.co/universe-manifestation-prayer/

Resto, W. (2021, May 15). *Surround yourself with people who encourage you to grow.*

Medium. https://medium.com/know-thyself-heal-thyself/surround-yourself-with-people-who-encourage-you-to-grow-9dc050d12e09

Rooney Armand, M. (2021, November 8). *How does faith impact your life? 10 inspiring examples of faithful living*. Butterfly Living. https://butterflyliving.org/how-does-faith-impact-your-life/

Russell, B. (2022, December 8). *7 classic Christian books for spiritual growth*. The Arc. https://www.tyndale.com/sites/readthearc/classic-christian-books-for-spiritual-growth/?srsltid=AfmBOooZ75DWT7lwk7TYH8_4lbabmkkSJjvvBPCNtOdmU6FBRUHYSeI5

Ryan, E. (2023, June 29). *Modern mentoring: Traditional mentors vs accountability partners*. Mentorloop Mentoring Software. https://mentorloop.com/blog/accountability-partners/

Scherer, J. S., Milazzo, K. C., Hebert, P. L., Engelberg, R. A., Lavallee, D. C., Vig, E. K., Kurella Tamura, M., Roberts, G., Curtis, J. R., & O'Hare, A. M. (2021, August 4). Association between self-reported importance of religious or spiritual beliefs and end-of-life care preferences among people receiving dialysis. *JAMA Network Open*. https://doi.org/10.1001/jamanetworkopen.2021.19355

Sims, K. D. (2024, June 7). *The Christian pocket guide to life: Conquer everyday life with these 20 Biblical passages, practical lessons, and spiritual insights*. Self-published.

Southwick, S. M., & Charney, D. S. (2018). *Resilience: The science of mastering life's greatest challenges*. Cambridge University Press.

Srock, J. (2023, December 5). *How to develop your spiritual formation plan*. Jonathan Srock. https://jonathansrock.com/how-to-develop-your-spiritual-formation-plan/

Stange, J. (2020, December 7). *Making plans that align with God's greater purposes*. DesireJesus.com. https://desirejesus.com/blog/2020/12/7/making-plans-that-align-with-gods-greater-purposes

Stephen, O. (2023). *Okot Stephen—Assessments*. International Institute for Global Leadership. https://global-leadership.com/index.php/okot-stephen-assessments/

Sutton, J. (2019). *What is resilience and why is it important to bounce back?* PositivePsychology.com. https://positivepsychology.com/what-is-resilience/

Syverson, G. (2024, November 18). *The art of resilience: Strategies for overcoming setbacks and embracing change*. Medium. https://medium.com/@syversonsolution/the-art-of-resilience-strategies-for-overcoming-setbacks-and-embracing-change-6dd1dc8a6b30

Tarrants, T. A. (2018, December 8). *Discovering God's purpose for your life*. C.S. Lewis Institute. https://www.cslewisinstitute.org/resources/discovering-gods-purpose-for-your-life/

TerKeurst, L. (2022). *One way to actually guard your heart*. Proverbs 31 Ministries.

https://proverbs31.org/read/devotions/full-post/2022/10/11/one-way-to-actu
ally-guard-your-heart

Thomas, B. (2024, February 20). *Top 7 benefits of community service in society.* Catchafire. https://blog.catchafire.org/community-service-benefits

3 positive affirmations to boost resilience. (2025, January 2). Rize OC Mental Health. https://rizeoc.com/3-positive-affirmations-to-boost-resilience/

Top 100 goals for your vision board: Faith and spirituality. (2023, October 4). Live Your Dream Board. https://liveyourdreamboard.com/top-100-goals-for-faith-and-spir
ituality/?srsltid=AfmBOoqEfaky93k-AA-w1ESDiJkjRLVawiqyca45hI5XjF09B9-
sRbxZ

Tozer, A. W. (2017). *The knowledge of the holy.* Fig Tree Books.

Whitman, L. (2023, November 20). *Daily spirituality and faith practices: Integrating everyday faith into routine.* MemoryCherish. https://memorycherish.com/daily-
spirituality/

Why did God create us? Why are we here? (n.d.). GotQuestions.org. https://www.
gotquestions.org/why-did-God-create-us.html

Wong, D. (2025, February 11). *Financial literacy for teens: 9 key concepts.* Daniel Wong. https://www.daniel-wong.com/2025/02/11/financial-literacy-for-teens/

Wright, K. W. (2023, May 4). *Reflective journal: Inspiration, ideas, and prompts.* Day One. https://dayoneapp.com/blog/reflective-journal/

www.ingramcontent.com/pod-product-compliance
Lightning Source LLC
Chambersburg PA
CBHW062050270326
41931CB00013B/3020